CUNARD

THE MOST FAMOUS OCEAN LINERS IN THE WORLD™

simple flower
arranging

simple flower arranging

MARK WELFORD & STEPHEN WICKS

London, New York, Munich,
Melbourne, Delhi

Project Editor Susannah Steel
Photography Carolyn Barber
Senior Art Editor Karen Constanti
Designer Mandy Earey
Managing Editor Dawn Henderson
Managing Art Editor Christine Keilty
Senior Jackets Creative Nicola Powling
Category Publisher Peggy Vance
Art Director Peter Luff
Pre-production Producer Raymond Williams
Senior Producer Oliver Jeffreys
Creative Technical Support
Sonia Charbonnier

First published in Great Britain in 2014
by Dorling Kindersley Limited
80 Strand London, WC2R 0RL

A Penguin Random House Company

2 4 6 8 10 9 7 5 3 1

Copyright © 2014 Dorling Kindersley

A CIP catalogue record for this book
is available from the British Library.
ISBN 978-1-4093-3735-5

Printed and bound by South China

Discover more at **www.dk.com/crafts**

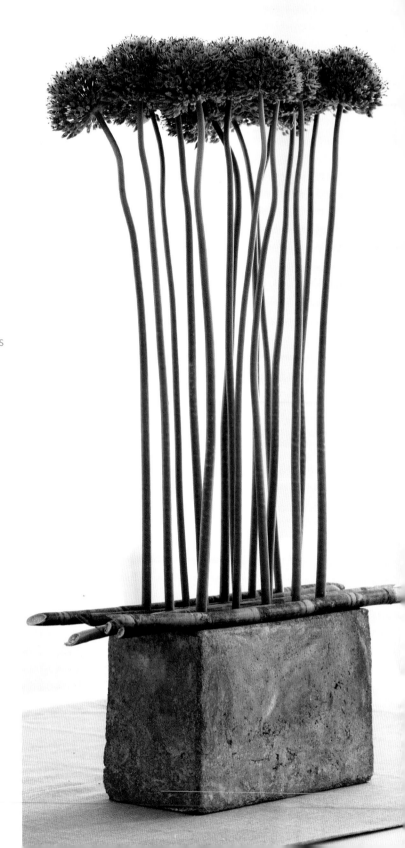

Contents

Foreword

Twenty years after retiring as dancers from the Royal Ballet and embarking on our second careers as floral designers, we are still constantly inspired by the variety of flowers, foliage, and plants available. Every year, growers create a new rose, tulip, or cut flower of interest, which helps us to keep our ideas fresh and evolve new designs. So when we were approached by DK to write a second book, we couldn't resist the chance to continue our mission of floral inspiration. Three years on from the publication of 'Flower Arranging', our basic principles – choose seasonal flowers and foliage when you can, use a container that suits the occasion, and less is more – remain the same, but our designs have progressed.

Whenever we are asked which is our favourite flower, it reminds us of another often-asked question: What were our best-loved dance roles? As a dancer, your preferred role is often defined by how far you have developed in your career. As florists, our favourite flower invariably changes, and is sparked by the anticipation of a change of season. As summer draws to a close, we include sunflowers and hydrangeas in our shop displays, and then amaryllis and foliage laden with berries in winter. The onset of spring heralds an abundance of tulips and planted bulbs to use, and in summer we ensure we always have enough frothy peonies and fragrant sweet peas. Many flowers these days are bred for their looks and longevity rather than their scent, but scent can be evocative and sensual, so we include scented ingredients, including herbs such as rosemary, whenever the season allows. While most flowers are fragile, and should always be handled with care, we make a point of creating designs that look enticing so that people want to reach out and touch them. We achieve this by mixing different flowers and foliage to create interesting textures, or using a quirky colour combination, or working with one variety of flower en masse.

Like a cook building up a collection of pans and baking tins over time, we believe it's important to source a selection of containers so you always have the right one for a specific design in a particular room. A geometric or sculptural container will suit a minimalist décor, for example, while a formal dining room may need something grander, such as a classical urn. We enhance our collection by looking in junk shops and flea markets, where we may find that one-off vintage pot or vase, and visiting large department stores, which hold selections of basic glassware. We also transform some items into containers that you may already have in your home to create interesting and unusual displays.

We do not necessarily adhere to strict guidelines of standard floristry principles about proportion, shape, and form, as we prefer to gauge these elements by eye. This is always influenced by where the design will be placed, the size of the container, and the flowers and foliage. We advocate putting your measuring tape aside and having fun working with your ingredients. We hope that you will learn, as we have, that often shape and form are all about proportion and what is pleasing to the eye.

We hope you enjoy this book, which covers a range of achievable designs, from basic displays to more creative arrangements. We have added a twist to each to make it a little different, whether it's the container, an unusual combination of flowers, or a decorative touch of seagrass cord. Take time to explore the many different designs and be inspired by this window into our work, which epitomizes our ethos and passion for this challenging, but rewarding, career.

Mark Welford & Stephen Wicks

Mark (left), and Stephen, and scenes from their shop, Bloomsbury Flowers, in Covent Garden, London.

Getting started

This short introduction is a condensed know-how of where to begin with simple flower arranging. It includes some of the theory to how we work and what informs our approach to flower design, and also explains some general plant care information and what equipment you will need. With this knowledge base, you can try the basic techniques at the beginning of each of the following chapters, before going on to master each different arrangement.

Colour palette

The colour scheme of an arrangement is probably the first thing you notice about it, and some flower colours simply work better together than others. Here is a brief guide to displaying your flowers to their full potential.

greens   whites   yellows   oranges

In colour theory, primary colours – red, blue, and yellow – can be mixed in different combinations to create a spectrum of other colours. Here, these colours are arranged in a line to show how they work in relation to each other. Colours that sit next to one another, such as purple and blue, are similiar, and are known as harmonious. Colours that sit far from each other are complementary: they enhance each other to look almost better together than apart. Blue and orange are complementary colours, as are purple and yellow, and red and green. Each colour also has tonal values – light and dark versions of the hue – which influence the mood of a design, making it warm or cool, gentle or intense. White can dominate a scheme, so white or cream flowers look best on their own, or with green flowers and foliage. Limit yourself to three or four harmonious colours or two complementary colours for the best results.

reds   pinks   purples   blues

Four essential vases

Before you buy any flowers, look at the space in which you plan to stand your arrangement and think about what kind of design you would like. Every flower display must suit its surroundings and the occasion, not only with the right choice of flower colours, but also in its shape, size, and style – which is all influenced by the container it sits in. This limited selection of vases represents the four basic shapes you need to create a huge variety of designs. We use all these vase shapes in this book in several different sizes, so it's worth thinking about buying large and small versions for a versatile vase collection.

Flared vase

Flowers and foliage fall naturally into an attractive fan shape in a flared vase, as its tapered base limits the spread of their stems. As a result, they stand more upright in the vase to give a sense of height and impact. This vase is ideal for both compact bouquets and a variety of flowers in a large arrangement, as you can see the individual blooms clearly.

Fish bowl vase

A multi-tasking vase, this globe shape is good for highlighting the beauty of just a few blooms curled inside the bowl, displaying tall-stemmed hand-tied bouquets that require a dramatic flare, or floating individual flower heads in water.

Column vase

With its tall straight sides, this vase "contains" the flowers or plants within it. Use it to give a sense of height to an arrangement, support long-stemmed flowers, or create a micro-climate for plants. It is also useful for contemporary and sculptural designs, or try using it instead of a traditional urn for a modern interpretation on a classic flower design.

Cube vase

The straight sides of this square-shaped vase enforce a geometric framework onto flowers and foliage, giving them a modern edge. Display small compact designs with short-stemmed flowers or a mass of one ingredient in several of these vases arranged in a line for visual impact.

Container collection

Collect a range of vases and containers so you always have an appropriate container to suit your design and surroundings. If, on occasion, you can't find something suitable, consider the option of using floral foam (pp144–85), or arrange your flowers as a hand-tied bouquet (pp32–63) and place them in a glass vase.

↙ Wine bottle
Use as it is, or spray-paint first, and use for single long-stemmed flowers or branches.

'Warwick' metal urn ↓
Use with floral foam for a classic display of flowers and foliage.

Snakegrass jam jar ↘
Customize a standard jam jar for an individual look.

↓ Terracotta pot
A rustic outdoor pot adds extra texture and colour.

↓ Tea gl...
Buy a selec...
of tea glass...
different co...
for informa...
displays.

Recycled bottle ↘
The attractive green hint of colour in recycled glass works well with minimalist foliage designs.

Eggcup ↑
Use for individual place settings or intimate displays.

↑ Tin can
Ideal for informal designs of just one or two ingredients.

↑ Teacup and saucer
Match the colours of the flowers you use to the design on the cup.

↑ Scent bottle
Use as part of a larger display or add just a few stems of one variety of flower.

Galvanized ↑ bucket
Buy several and fill each with a small potted plant.

Birch bark-covered vase with seagrass ↓
Disguise a column vase with natural materials for an interesting look.

↓ **Ornamental bottle**
This tall bottle sets off long-stemmed single ingredients beautifully.

Glazed pottery vase ↓
A rough-textured vase is useful for bouquets, whether hand tied or loosely arranged.

↓ **Glazed antique pot**
The deep hue of this opaque vase suits displays with a strong colour scheme.

Hydrangea leaf-covered pot ↓
Disguise or reinvent a vase or pot with a lining or wrapping of fresh leaves.

Coir pot ↑
These fibre pots are good for potted bulbs; don't let them get too wet or they disintegrate.

↑ **Antique bowl**
The classic shape and texture of this bowl suits traditional arrangements.

Clay pot ↑
Use for simple, informal, rustic flower and potted plant displays.

Jam jar ↑
Keep it simple for low-key displays, or add raffia or ribbons around the neck for a celebratory effect.

↑ **Preserving jar**
Large preserving or storage jars make great containers for potted plants.

↑ **Cheese pot**
For a simple, rustic, instant container for a plant, use the base of a wooden cheese pot.

Flower shapes

The enormously diverse flower varieties available can be condensed into a limited range of basic shapes. Recognizing these shapes is extremely helpful in understanding how different flowers work best in arrangements. The eight flower shapes displayed here are those that we think are among the most attractive and useful for flower arranging.

Flat-topped (trachelium) →
Most flat-topped flowers are quite large, but the many tiny flowers arranged in clusters on short stalks that form these flower heads make them airy and delicate in appearance.
Good for This flower shape is useful for hand-tied bouquets, as it helps to form the required dome shape. It also provides textural interest and detail in both large and small designs.
Flowers Trachelium, Queen Anne's lace (cow parsley), bouvardia, sedum

Rosette (rose) →
The geometric rosette shape of some flowers makes them ideal for both large and small flower arrangements.
Good for These flowers attract the eye easily, so they can be used as feature flowers in a mixed display or on their own in a minimalist design.
Flowers Single roses, dahlias, ranunculus, peonies, carnations

← **Regular (gerbera)**
Flowers with the same shaped petals in a simple circular shape around its centre have radial symmetry: whichever way you divide a regular flower, it has two or three similar parts.
Good for These flowers are adaptable: they can be used on their own in striking designs or as a repeat pattern in a larger arrangement.
Flowers Gerberas, germinis, sunflowers, chrysanthemums

Dome (hydrangea) →
Large and small domed flowers provide substance and focus in an arrangement. The flower heads are usually quite dense and provide a strong injection of colour in a design.
Good for This flower shape is suitable for large displays and minimalist designs.
Flowers Hydrangeas, brassicas, allium 'Schubertii', most celosias

← Globe (allium)
The perfectly round shape of globe flowers means they look most impressive en masse, and usually work best in a minimalist design of just one or two types of flower.
Good for These flowers work well in modern and sculptural designs, especially if the strong, straight stems of flowers such as alliums are left as long as possible.
Flowers Alliums, tulips, protea

Spray (eryngium) →
With their branching stems and large quantity of flower heads, spray flowers are adaptable, and ideal for mixed flower arrangements.
Good for If the flower heads are left on their single main stem, they can be used to reinforce the fan shape of a vase display, or provide a mass of colour and interest in hand-tied bouquets. They can also be cut down to provide numerous shorter-stemmed flowers in floral foam designs.
Flowers Lilies, spray roses, lisianthus, astrantia, gypsophila

← Spear (delphinium)
Clusters of small flowers on short stalks growing at the top of a stem form a typical spear flower shape. With so many individual flowers on one stem, these flowers are full of colour and interest.
Good for Flowers with elongated stems, such as delphiniums, provide structure, form, and necessary height in large vases or structural designs.
Flowers Delphiniums, eremurus, gladioli

Spire (veronica) →
A spire shape has small, stalkless flowers at the tip of a long stem. The flowers open in sequence, usually from the bottom, which helps to create its tapering shape.
Good for These shapes contrast well with softer-petalled flowers, and are useful for breaking the smooth outlines of a domed bouquet or floral foam design.
Flowers Lily of the valley, lavender, stocks

Foliage

The aim of adding foliage to an arrangement is to provide texture, extra colour, shape, and proportion. It can also help to give a design necessary height, width, depth, and interest to make it look balanced and substantial. The foliage you choose will depend on its seasonal or all-year availability.

All-year foliage

With the exception of ruscus, all-year foliage tends to be short, and so is best used for medium-sized and compact arrangements. Choose foliage such as pittosporum, salal gaultheria, eucalyptus, bear grass, snake grass, leather leaf, and black tie and green tie leaves.

← **Ruscus**
These attractive feathery leaves on long curved stems add a delicate texture to a design.

Salal →
This foliage is a dense filler, best used for small designs and bouquets.

Eucalyptus →
The unusual silver-green leaves, pleasant scent, and handsome arching stems of eucalyptus enhance the shape of a design and add an extra flourish.

Seasonal foliage

The tall, straight stems of cotinus, forsythia, privet, red robin, white leaf, and rhododendron are ideal for large displays, and any side shoots can be used at the edges of a design, or in a compact arrangement. Hebe, berried ivy, senecio, hypericum, and alchemilla are best suited for compact arrangements. Condition seasonal foliage well, or it will quickly droop.

Alchemilla mollis →
With its unusual lime-green colour and lacy appearance, alchemilla is ideal for breaking up a dense mass of flowers. It is pretty enough to be used like a flower in some designs.

Red robin ↓
This red-stemmed foliage adds a rich colour accent to an autumn display.

← Privet
Tall and dramatic, privet provides an effective backdrop for long-stemmed flowers. .

Equipment

To prepare, arrange, and maintain the simplest of flower displays, you need just a few essentials: florist's scissors, secateurs, a hand mister, string or raffia to tie bouquets, sterilizing tablets for clear glass vases, and a large bucket to condition the flowers and foliage. Here, we have also included other pieces of useful kit that you will need to make the arrangements in this book, and more.

Florist's tape ↓
Use to bind floral foam to a plastic tray or bowl.

Sticky tape ↓
Use to bind split stems, make grids across vase tops, and wrap bouquets.

Stem tape ↓
Use to cover and seal individually wired flower and foliage stems.

Hand mister ↓
Use to refresh or revive blooms with a fine mist of water.

← **Sterilizing tablets**
Add to a clear glass vase or container of water to help keep the water clear and kill all bacteria.

← **Paintbrush**
For dusting any pollen off flower petals.

↑ **Green tack**
Use to attach materials to containers.

↑ **Posy bowl**
Shallow plastic bowl designed to hold enough floral foam for a small arrangement.

Pin cushion ↓
Necessary for arranging stems at precise angles.

↑ **Bottle brush**
For cleaning vases and containers.

← **Deep bowl**
Plastic bowl that holds enough floral foam to make up a large front-facing display.

Pearl pins ↑
For buttonholes and pinning ribbons in place.

← Garden canes in various sizes

Useful for providing support and placing various ingredients in position.

Raffia ↓

Ideal for binding hand-tied bouquets and arranged stems together.

Garden string ↓

A suitable alternative to raffia. Also try twine.

Chicken wire ↓

Mould to fit and place in an opaque vase or container to hold the stems of an arrangement in place.

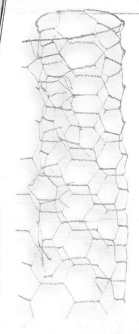

Plastic bottle ↑

Cut-down plastic bottle to hold flowers in water in non-watertight containers.

Rose wires →

Use for wiring smaller-stemmed flowers and buttonholes.

↓ Long phial

Attach to short-stemmed flowers in mixed designs.

↑ Decorative coloured reel wires

Wires of various thickness to bind flower stems or add decorative details.

22 gauge wire →

Suitable for wiring larger flower stems, ribbons, and other equipment.

Elastic bands ↑

Useful for making up bunches of finer foliage such as bear grass.

Floral foam block and tray →

Use for medium-sized floral foam arrangements.

Craft knife →

Use to condition flowers and cut and trim soaked blocks of floral foam.

Short phial ↓

For keeping single-stemmed flowers fresh before being presented.

← Secateurs ·

Use to trim and split woody-stemmed foliage and thick-stemmed flowers.

↑ Florist's scissors

Ideal for conditioning and trimming flowers and thin-stemmed foliage.

Maintenance and tips

Flowers and foliage benefit hugely from being conditioned, or prepared, properly before they are arranged, as they will look fresher and last longer. Cleaning the vase or container properly first, and keeping the water clean and fresh, makes a difference too. We've also included several useful tips to help you keep your flowers looking their absolute best while on display.

Use a bottle brush to clean a vase or container thoroughly, as you can angle it into awkward corners to lift out dirt and bacteria.

Make a diagonal cut about 2.5cm (1in) from the base of each stem, and split any woody stems.

Clean the container

Whenever you use a vase or a container filled with water to display your arrangement, bacteria will build up, particularly in the corners of the container. This bacteria can kill the flowers, shortening their life dramatically. Wear washing-up gloves and use hot water, washing-up liquid, a touch of bleach, and a bottle brush to clean the container thoroughly either before or after each use to get rid of all bacteria.

Condition flowers and foliage

Select the best-quality flowers and foliage you can find and condition them as soon as possible after buying or cutting them. Strip excess leaves from the stems, and split the ends of any woody stems with florist's scissors or secateurs, to encourage the stems to take up more water and hydrate the flowers. Fewer leaves will also encourage more buds to open. Stand the stems in a bucket of deep, cool water for about an hour before re-cutting and re-splitting the stems and arranging the ingredients.

• Depending on the occasion and how quickly you want a display to look its best, choose blooms that are either still in bud or just beginning to open. If you buy peonies in tight bud, you can encourage them to open quickly by misting them once a day.

• As well as cleaning your vases and containers, it's worth giving the buckets that you use to condition your flowers and foliage a good scrub occasionally.

Clean stems without leaves below the waterline look sophisticated and help to keep the water clear.

Allow the sterilizing tablet to dissolve completely before adding any flowers or foliage to the vase.

Add a sterilizing tablet

If you use a clear glass vase, drop a sterilizing tablet into the water first and let it dissolve. The tablet will help to keep the water clear, making the arrangement look more attractive and eliminating any odour. It also prevents the build-up of bacteria. You can add a sterilizing tablet to every water-filled vase if you want to kill off bacteria, but it's not imperative if you change the water every two or three days. Look in a pharmacy for sterilizing tablets (not water purification tablets) that are suitable for sterilizing baby equipment.

No foliage below the waterline

Although you will have stripped off any excess leaves before conditioning your flowers and foliage, you will probably need to remove more leaves before adding the stems to a vase or container. Hold each stem against the side of the container and strip off any leaves that would otherwise sit below the waterline. This makes it easier to arrange the stems, prevents the water turning murky quickly, and keeps the appearance of the stems looking clean and neat if you use a clear glass vase.

Cut a slit about 2.5cm (1in) long in the neck of the tulip.

Hold the calla lily stem between your thumb and forefinger and massage it gently.

Slit tulip stems

Tulips continue to grow after they have been cut – about 2.5cm (1in) a night – if left in water. Try this tip to halt the growth of the flowers so they don't spoil or alter the shape of an arrangement. Place each tulip on a flat surface and use a craft knife to carefully slit the centre of the stem lengthways just under the flower head.

Massage calla lily stems

For any arrangement that includes curved calla lily stems, first massage each stem gently with your thumb and forefinger. This will help to break down the fibres inside the stem of the flower, and encourage the stem to bend so the head droops slightly. Don't massage the stem too firmly, or you may crush it.

Submerge the hydrangea flower head in the water; its petals are robust enough not to turn slimy.

• Many woody-stemmed flowers, such as lilac and roses, can be revived by immersing the stems in boiling water. Pour 10cm (4in) of boiling water into a bucket, re-cut the ends of the stems, stand them in the water for up to 45 seconds, and then transfer them to fresh, cool water.

• Revive discoloured moss by placing it in a sink and pouring a kettle of boiling water over it. The moss should instantly look greener.

Gently pull out the individual pollen-laden stamens from the centre of each flower as it starts to open.

Hydrangea care

If your hydrangea flowers begin to wilt while on display, fill a large vase or bucket with cold water and plunge the hydrangea flowers headfirst into the water for 30 minutes. Then re-cut and split the stems, replace the water in the vase or container, and insert the flowers back into the arrangement.

Remove lily pollen

To prevent allergy sufferers from experiencing any symptoms, and to avoid unsightly pollen stains on lily or other flower petals, or on clothing or furniture, carefully remove the pollen sacs in the lilies before the sacs open. Gently pull out the stamens that carry the pollen with your thumb and forefinger, or cut them out using a pair of scissors. Use a paintbrush to dust off any pollen that accidentally falls onto any petals. It is worth noting that lily pollen is poisonous to cats and dogs.

Arrangement choosers

The right combination of flowers and foliage in a limited palette of colours, arranged in an interesting way in a stylish container, will instantly impact your senses. This selection of arrangements, which are all featured in the book, are grouped into particular colour schemes to show how the basic principles of colour, shape, and form together communicate a particular mood or image.

Bright and sunny

Yellow and orange are both bold, saturated colours, and work well together to give a dramatic impact. To create an intense shot of colour, arrange the flowers on their own without foliage in a vase or as a hand-tied bouquet, for example. To break and soften these strong colours, mix them with foliage and other, more subtle, coloured flowers in a large arrangement.

Fresh and cool

Green and white, or cream, impart a clean, serene mood. These colours are a classic combination that makes every arrangement look classy and wonderful, whether minimalist and sculptural or soft and pretty. They suit any environment, and are a fail-safe neutral combination if you want to give flowers as a gift and don't know where the arrangement will be placed, or what would suit the room décor. There are plenty of green and white flowers and foliage available throughout the year to make an attractive display.

Bold and intense

Pink and red flowers are a modern, quite
challenging combination; when mixed
together, they are powerfully concentrated
and conspicuous. On their own, these rich
colours also work as a strong, confident
statement. Grouping pink flowers on their
own works whether you mix a range of pastel
and bright pinks, or choose just one pink
shade for a more intense display. Red flowers
can sometimes look a little flat on their own,
but if you group a selection of different
shades of red blooms together (pp58–9),
they become more exciting and vibrant.

Calm and deep

Soothing hues of blue and purple are a perfect summer combination; most varieties of blue and purple flowers are available during the summer months. Together they convey a sense of peaceful tranquillity, spaciousness, and serenity. Lilac – essentially a pastel mix of blue and purple hues – works especially well with blue and purple, or used en masse on its own. Strong purple, although a striking statement colour, suits a sculptural arrangement if used individually, while blue mixed with green foliage makes a beautifully harmonious display.

Bouquets

The most popular design in our shop, bouquets are a beautiful way to present flowers either as a gift or in a vase. In most instances, the same spiral-stem technique is used to create a structured shape, whether compact or loose, and it is the diversity of flowers in successful colour combinations and carefully chosen containers that creates variety and impact.

White and green hand tie

Loose and informal in style with a deliberately minimalist colour palette, this bouquet is arranged using a straightforward but impressive-looking spiral technique. The "binding point", where the flowers are tied, is fairly high so they sit beautifully in the vase.

signature details

The soft country look of this bouquet is determined by its harmonious green, white, and creamy yellow colour scheme and the fact that it doesn't contain stems of foliage (alchemilla mollis is used here as a variety of flower); foliage in a bouquet produces a sharper, more striking look. As with all our mixed bouquets, no two flowers of the same variety sit next to each other; they are all evenly dispersed throughout the arrangement. The absence of leaves below the waterline, and the stylish swirl of clean stems that results from using a spiral technique, are aesthetic details that help to lift and refine this design.

flowers

White → stock

↓ Alchemilla mollis

↓ Camomile

↑ Green hypericum

Guelder rose ↑

← White rose

you will need

7 green hypericum
7 white stocks
9 alchemilla mollis
9 white roses
6 camomile
5 guelder rose

materials

Florist's scissors
Garden string, twine, or raffia
1 large clear glass fish bowl vase

for step by step, see overleaf

White and green hand tie
step by step

The binding point is where you hold the stems and tie the bouquet. The higher the binding point, the more compact the design.

The flower heads sit about 15cm (6in) above this binding point. Any leaves below the binding point should have been stripped off.

1 Hold 1 hypericum stem and place 5 alchemilla and 4 more hypericum around it, adding 1 stem of each variety in turn. Angle the stems slightly as you arrange them.

2 Add a rose, inserting it at an angle into the bunch where your thumb rests, so the stem points towards you and the flower points away. Turn the bunch slightly in one direction. Repeat with 2 more roses.

3 Intersperse 5 stems of camomile at the same angle around the outside of the bouquet. Turn the bunch slightly after adding each flower. Then twist the bunch round to face you – or hold it in front of a mirror – to spot any obvious gaps and check you are happy with the distribution of blooms so far. Adjust a few flowers slightly if needed.

Hold the bunch at the binding point with your left hand if you are right-handed, and vice versa if you are left-handed.

insider tips

• Strip all the leaves from their stems below the binding point before you start arranging. This makes the bouquet easier to hold as you build it, prevents leaves sitting below the waterline and turning the water murky, and gives the stems a clean look.

• Arrange the different flowers (and foliage, if using) into separate piles before you start so you can pick up each variety in turn to distribute the flowers properly.

• Turn the bunch slightly in the same direction after you add each stem to create the correct spiral stem effect.

4 Add 3 stems of guelder rose, working the stems into the centre as well as around the edges. Guelder rose naturally curves down, enhancing the rounded shape of this bouquet.

The spiral of stems should now be evident. Roughly trim the stems if the bunch becomes top-heavy, but don't trim them too short.

5 Add 5 stocks, then add one more of each bloom around them, angling these flowers slightly lower around the edges of the bunch to build its rounded shape. Check the look of the bouquet from the top again.

6 Angle the remaining flowers so they sit even lower around the edges to complete the domed shape. Secure the bouquet at the binding point with garden string, twine, or raffia and tie in a knot. Trim the stems into a neat curve, cutting each end at an angle.

Red and pink hand tie

With its high binding point and absence of leaves and foliage, this compact modern bouquet draws the eye straight to a fabulous riot of iridescent pink and rich red flowers and the intricate shapes and textures of their petals. These flowers should last for five to seven days.

flowers

↓ Red celosia   ↓ Pink aqua rose

↓ Red 'Grand Prix' rose

→ Pink celosia

← Strong pink dahlia

how to arrange

1 Divide the flowers into separate piles. Hold the stem of 1 red celosia in your hand, about 10cm (4in) below the flower head, and arrange 1 of each of the other flowers around it. Turn the bunch slightly in one direction after adding each stem.

2 Insert 1 pink aqua or red 'Grand Prix' rose at an angle into the bunch at the point where your thumb rests, so the end of the stem points towards you and the flower head points away. Add 1 more of each of the other flowers at the same angle to create a spiral stem effect. Continue to turn the bunch round in the same direction after adding each flower.

3 Look at the top of the bouquet to check you like the arrangement of blooms and adjust any if necessary. Insert the last few layers of flowers a little lower around the edges and at a more acute angle so they create a domed effect.

4 Secure the bunch at the binding point using garden string or twine tied in a knot, and trim the stems to neaten them, then cut each stem at an angle.

 *insider tips*

• Use a high binding point to create a compact bouquet with the flowers set very close together for more impact. This will ensure that there are no gaps between the flower heads and that their petals almost merge into one another.

• Choose a rustic, pale-coloured ceramic vase for the bouquet. Replace the water after three days and re-cut the stems of the flowers to prolong their life.

you will need

6 pink aqua roses
6 red 'Grand Prix' roses
3 pink celosias
3 red celosias
9 strong-pink dahlias

materials

Florist's scissors
Garden string or twine

Orange and yellow hand tie

Small and compact, but full of texture, this hand-tied bouquet is all the more striking for its absence of foliage. The effect is of a mass of vibrantly coloured fresh flowers bursting open at the same time. Use a spiral stem technique to create the domed effect (pp36–37).

how to arrange

1 Remove all leaves from the stems below the binding point. Hold the stem of a haemanthus in your hand and arrange 1 stem of each variety of flower around it.

2 Insert a freesia at an angle into the bunch, at the point where your thumb rests, so the end of the stem points towards you and the flower head points away. Turn the bunch slightly in one direction before adding more flowers alternately at the same angle. Turn the bunch in the same direction after adding each flower to create a spiral stem effect. Every so often, look at the design from above to check the different flowers are evenly distributed.

3 Arrange the last two layers of flowers a little lower around the edges of the bouquet to produce a domed effect.

4 Secure the bunch with a length of garden string or twine tied firmly in a knot.

5 Cut the stems' ends straight across with scissors so they are all the same length and place in a vase of water, then top the vase up with more water.

 insider tips

• Use a high binding point – about 10cm (4in) below the flower heads – to keep the spiral effect tight and ensure there are no gaps between the flowers.

• This compact design looks best in a small roughly textured vase, so cut the spiralled stems as short as necessary for the bouquet to fit in the vase. The flowers should last for one week if you change the water every two days.

flowers

Yellow rose →

Orange ranunculus ↓

Yellow freesia →

Orange → haemanthus

↑ Orange ornithogalum

you will need

10 orange ranunculus
15 yellow freesias
10 orange haemanthus
15 orange ornithogalum
6 yellow roses

materials

Florist's scissors
Garden string or twine

Vibrant combination

The yellow and orange flowers in this small bouquet are all chosen for their saturated, bold colour. Touches of lime green in the sepals and unopened buds add an extra hint of bright colour that blends into the other hues.

Purple and blue hand tie

Rich blue, pale lilac, and deep purple garden flowers with green foliage together create an abundant, harmonious vision of early summer. Place this bouquet in a roughly hewn jar or vase for a rustic look and sit it where you can inhale the heavenly fragrance of lilac as you pass by.

how to arrange

1 Sort the different flowers and foliage into separate piles and strip off all leaves that will be below the binding point (see tip, below). Hold the stem of a large flower, such as an allium, in your hand at the binding point and arrange a stem of each different foliage and flower around it.

2 Add 1 stem of each flower and foliage in turn (so that no varieties sit together), inserting each at an angle into the bunch at the point where your thumb rests, so the end of the stem points towards you and the flower head points away. This helps to create a spiral stem effect. Twist the bunch round slightly in one direction in your hand before adding the next stem.

3 Intermittently, look at the top of the bouquet to check you like the arrangement of blooms and adjust them slightly if necessary. Arrange the last two layers of flowers and foliage a little lower around the edges to create a domed effect.

4 Tie the bunch at the binding point with garden string or twine secured in a knot.

5 Using secateurs, trim the stems at an angle so they are the same length and can all sit in water. The flowers will last for five days if you change the water every day.

insider tips

• Lilac is woody, so split the stems with secateurs before you arrange them.

• Use a medium binding point for this design so the arranged flowers will look fairly loose; hold each stem about 12cm (5in) below the flower head.

flowers and foliage

Purple allium ↓

Short blue ↓ delphinium

Centaurea ↓

Garden lilac ↓

← Eucalyptus parvifolia

↑ Veronica

you will need

5 garden lilac
10 short blue delphiniums
9 purple alliums
7 veronica
5 eucalyptus parvifolia stems
7 centaurea

materials

Florist's scissors
Secateurs
Garden string or twine

Presentation sheaf

A sheaf is a variation on a hand-tied bouquet, revealing the flowers and foliage in an elongated layered effect rather than a rounded format. It is a classic, rather romantic arrangement that can be presented as a gift or reduced slightly in size and used as a wedding bouquet.

flowers

← Cream stock

↓ Peach rose

Cream ↓
lisianthus

↓ Guelder
rose

Magnolia ↑
leaf stem

← Eucalyptus
parvifolia

signature details

The elegance of this arrangement lies in the graduated layering of each variety of flower, drawing your eye from lime green and cream flowers resting on dark, lush foliage at the top of the design down to a group of peach roses massing on top of the other flowers just above the binding point. The flowers are tied in a grand knot with a large "hank" of raffia to add another element of natural texture, and any leaves below the binding point are stripped from their stems to complete the refined look.

you will need

2 cream lisianthus
5 cream stocks
5–6 peach roses
3 guelder rose
3 magnolia stems
3 eucalyptus parvifolia stems

materials

Florist's scissors
Garden string or twine
A hank, or bunch, of raffia

for step by step, see overleaf

Presentation sheaf
step by step

Arrange the two types of foliage first, creating a slightly rounded framework on which to lay the different varieties of flowers.

1 Place the 3 magnolia stems on a flat surface and cross the stems over in the same place. Arrange the more delicate eucalyptus stems on top of them.

2 Arrange the 3 guelder rose stems on top of the foliage. Graduate the flowers down the arrangement slightly, so the foliage can still be seen at the top.

3 Layer the lisianthus in between and just below the guelder rose. Strip any lower leaves from the stocks and sit them slightly below the lisianthus.

Cross the stems of foliage about halfway down their stems to produce quite a loose bouquet with a medium binding point.

Cross the stems of the guelder rose at the same point over those of the foliage to keep the same binding point.

insider tips

• Lisianthus is branched, so trim it down to individual stems (two long stems can be cut down to six shorter stems) before arranging.

• Once presented, the bouquet can be taken apart and arranged in a vase of water; trim the longer stems if necessary.

• If you want to give this arrangement as a sympathy bouquet, take three long stems of rosemary (a symbol of remembrance), strip off two-thirds of the leaves, and tuck the stems in between the roses just above the binding point.

4 Arrange the roses in a layered cluster just above the binding point, angling the stems so they echo the outline of the magnolia leaves at the top of the bouquet.

The roses are a main feature of this bouquet; choose almost fully opened peach roses for the best effect.

5 Secure the arrangement tightly at the binding point with a length of twine, string, or a couple of lengths of raffia. Tie in a firm knot and cut off the loose ends.

6 Cover the secured binding point with a hank of raffia tied in an informal knot. Trim the stems into a gentle curve that echoes the outline of the bouquet's foliage, cutting each stem at an angle.

Exotic bouquet

The long-lasting, richly coloured tropical flowers in this spiral stem design should remain in perfect condition for at least two weeks, so it is an excellent arrangement to give as a gift or place in an entrance hall or a busy area. Re-cut the stems and renew the water every four days.

how to arrange

1 Hold the stem of 1 anthurium in your hand and arrange 1 each of the other flower stems and the red robin around it, turning the bunch around slightly in one direction after adding each stem. Be careful when arranging the protea, as the flower heads can easily snap off.

2 Insert another anthurium stem at an angle into the bunch at the point where your thumb rests so the end of the stem points towards you and the flower head points away. Avoid touching the anthurium flower head, as it marks easily. Add 1 each of the other stems in succession, at the same angle, to create a spiral stem effect. Keep turning the bunch around in the same direction after you add each flower or stem of foliage.

3 Arrange the last layer of flowers and foliage a little lower around the edges of the bouquet for a slightly domed effect.

4 Holding the bunch in one hand, secure it with a length of garden string or twine and trim the ends of the stems with scissors so they are the same length.

insider tip

• Choose a highly textured vase – such as a column vase covered in birch bark secured in place with seagrass cord – to show off the fleshy smooth petals of the tropical anthurium, orchid, and heliconia.

flowers and foliage

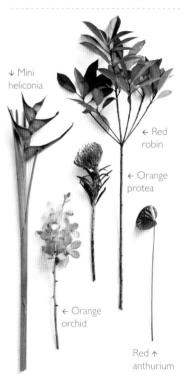

↓ Mini heliconia

← Red robin

← Orange protea

← Orange orchid

Red ↑ anthurium

you will need

6 red anthurium
5 orange orchids
3 orange protea
5 red robin
3 mini heliconia

materials

Florist's scissors
Garden string or twine

substitution

Pink orchids, pink protea, pink ginger lilies, and pink anthuriums to alter the colour scheme slightly

Fragrant herb nosegay

herbs

Camomile ↓

↓ Sage

↓ Flowering mint

↓ Marjoram

Mint →

← Rosemary

Like the nosegays traditionally carried by people to mask the smells of life in the street, this verdant herb posy imparts a fresh, uplifting fragrance. It lasts for four days.

how to arrange

1 Arrange the marjoram using a spiral stem technique with a high binding point (pp36–37), to create a rounded shape. Secure with twine and trim the stems to 15cm (6in). Repeat with the other bunches of herbs.

2 Gather the separate bunches together into one posy, spiralling the bunches together to create a domed effect. Tie the bunch with twine, keeping the binding point high so the bunches sit close together.

you will need

10 marjoram stems
4 camomile
5 rosemary stems
8 mint stems
8 flowering mint
5 sage stems
5 bay stems

materials

Florist's scissors
Garden string or twine

 insider tips

• Strip the leaves from the herbs below their binding point to give clean stems that are easy to handle when arranging.

• Display the nosegay in a slim ceramic vase. When you break up the display, stand the herbs in fresh water in the kitchen and use their leaves in cooking.

Mixed herbs

In terms of visual impact, most herbs can't compete with other flowers and foliage, but when gathered together in a small posy, their dainty flowers, and the texture and scent of their leaves, make a delightful display.

Tulip hand tie

A single variety of flower in just one or two hues creates a striking arrangement. This compact spiral hand tie of saturated red and peachy-orange tulips is set in a large pale, textured vase for maximum impact.

how to arrange

1 Strip off the leaves and slit the throat of each tulip to stop it growing (p26). Hold the stems of 2 red tulips just below their flower heads for a high binding point and place a group of 2–3 orange tulips against them at an angle. Turn the bunch slightly in one direction after adding these stems.

2 Add another group of 3 red tulips into the bunch at an angle at the place where your thumb rests, so the stems point towards you and the flowers point away. Turn the bunch again slightly in the same direction.

3 Add more small groups of orange and red tulips alternately, angling each at the same angle to create a spiral stem effect, and turning the bunch as you work. Angle the last flowers a little lower around the edges of the bunch to give a domed effect.

4 Secure the bouquet at the binding point with a length of twine, string, or raffia.

5 Fill the vase with water. Cut the ends of the stems so they are all the same length and place the bouquet in the vase.

insider tips

• Use a high binding point to keep the flower heads close together and the bouquet compact in appearance.

• Tulip stems are thick and a large quantity can be hard to hold in one hand, so tie off the bunch halfway through to make the bouquet manageable to arrange. Also trim the long floppy stems to make the bunch lighter and easier to hold.

• Choose a tall opaque vase with a small neck to show off the bouquet. Replace the water every two days so the flowers look fresh for at least a week.

flowers

Red tulip ↓

Orange tulip ↓

you will need

20–25 red tulips
20–25 orange tulips

materials

Craft knife
Florist's scissors
Garden string, twine, or raffia

substitution

Pink and red peonies

Grouped bouquet

For a fresh change from a classic bouquet, where the different flowers are evenly distributed, try this grouped bouquet. Four individual bunches of intensely red single flower varieties are tied together into a stunning square-shaped design that should last for up to a week.

flowers

Red spray rose →

Red dahlia ↓

↓ Red hydrangea

Red peony →

signature details

This modern, geometric bouquet achieves its novel look by drawing the eye to both the depth of textural detail and visual interest concentrated within each "quarter", and the appearance of the bouquet as a whole; from every angle, the different flower varieties enhance one another and yet look resplendent as a massed bunch of individual blooms. Set the arrangement off by displaying it in a column vase wrapped in birch bark and placed in a glass fishbowl.

you will need

2 hydrangeas
Approximately 12 dahlias, depending on
  the variety of dahlia
8 red spray roses
7 peonies

materials

Florist's scissors
Garden string or twine
1 large glass fish bowl vase
1 medium column vase
A few large pieces of birch bark

for step by step, see overleaf

Grouped bouquet
step by step

If the hydrangea heads are small, you may need to include more of these flowers and arrange them using a spiral stem technique.

1 Trim the hydrangea stems and tie them together with twine to create a medium binding point. The size of these large bunched flower heads is a "template" for the 3 bunches of smaller flowers.

2 Arrange the dahlias in a bunch using a spiral stem technique (pp36–37) and a medium binding point to give a gently domed shape. Turn the bunch in the same direction after you add each flower.

3 Check the size of the dahlia bouquet against the bunch of hydrangeas and add a few more stems if necessary. Then tie off the bunch with twine secured firmly in a knot.

Compare the size of the smaller flower heads against the bunched hydrangeas to gauge how many stems of each will match its size.

insider tip

• If you find it hard to hold all the individual bunches in one hand while you arrange them, tie two of the bunches together with twine and repeat with the other two bunches. Holding two slightly larger bunches should make it easier to tweak the four varieties into position.

With your hand holding all of the stems at the binding point, adjust the bunches to create a domed shape with slightly square edges.

4 Arrange the spray roses in the same way, using the spiral stem technique and a medium binding point. Check the bunch is the same size as the hydrangeas before tying it firmly with twine.

Strip almost all of the leaves from the stems – this should be all about the flowers with just a few flashes of green to enhance the red hues.

5 Arrange the peonies using the same spiral stem technique and binding point, and matching the size of the bunch to that of the hydrangeas. If your peonies are almost fully open, you may not need many flower stems.

6 Spiral the 4 bunches to create a domed bouquet. Secure them together with twine and cut across the ends of the stems to neaten them. Split the woody hydrangea stems at the same time (pp24–25) and the rose stems too.

Flowering dahlias

Up close, these dahlias become an extraordinary, almost sculptural, feature. They also reveal the change in colour saturation along the lengths of their numerous petals. Some dahlias have tall stems, so work well in vase displays.

Informal designs

This chapter is full of basic arrangements that are designed to give maximum impact. Most of the designs require the minimum of ingredients, and use everyday objects from your home as containers, to create a fresh take on simple flower arranging.

Flower and vegetable plate

This easy centrepiece for a kitchen or outdoor table mixes hydrangea heads, with their abundant petals, and delicate guelder rose with edible produce to create a playful yet stylish design with a tantalising array of textural detail. Use a minimal colour palette for impact.

signature details

This design is all about curves; there are no sharp angles or long pointed tips to be seen. Hydrangeas and broccoli, both domed varieties comprising lots of small florets, combine with globe-shaped guelder rose, garlic bulbs, and dusky purple figs to create a gently rounded shape. Texture is also a key element in this design, mixing smooth and irregular surfaces with layers of delicate petals. This is a good arrangement to try if you want to gain confidence in judging by eye how to place different elements together for the best effect.

flowers

Guelder → rose

Garlic bulbs ↓

← Purple figs

→ Sprouting broccoli, sweet stem broccoli, or broccoli florets

↑ White hydrangea

← Carpet moss

you will need

2 white hydrangeas
3 guelder rose
Carpet moss
1 packet of sprouting broccoli, sweet stem broccoli, or broccoli florets
6 figs
5 garlic bulbs

materials

30cm (12in) square of chicken wire
Green tack
1 plate with a deep lip, or shallow bowl

substitution

Purple trachelium instead of hydrangeas and plums or kiwi fruit instead of figs

for step by step, see overleaf

Flower and vegetable plate
step by step

Mould the large piece of sticky green tack into a ball and press it firmly onto the centre of the plate to hold the chicken wire in place.

Trim the hydrangea into smaller clusters if the flower heads look too large, but make sure their stems are long enough to sit in water.

I Fix the chicken wire to the plate with green tack. Pour water into the dish. Trim the stems of the broccoli, hydrangeas, and guelder rose to about 8cm (3in).

2 Arrange a few of the flowers, broccoli and some moss around the edge of the plate. Arrange the guelder rose within the chicken wire frame, as its curved stems need to be supported.

3 Build up the design in sections around the edge of the plate and working towards the centre. Restrict the moss to the rim of the plate so it sits in the water.

Mould the chicken wire roughly into the shape of a round bird's nest, tucking in any sharp ends, before securing it to the plate.

insider tips

• Green tack is extremely strong and also waterproof, so it is ideal for securing the chicken wire to the plate and holding it in place.

• Use a large ceramic plate with a deep lip as your base, as it will need to hold a few centimetres of water.

• The arrangement should last for a week, but replace any ingredients if they look tired or have lost their colour, and refresh the water every day.

You may need to remove the broccoli stems and cut them shorter if they rise up from the arrangement too obviously.

4 Cover the exposed chicken wire with ingredients, inserting the stems through the framework and down into the water. Check that none of the stems are out of water.

5 Gently rest the garlic bulbs on top of the chicken frame, interspersing them around the domed arrangement so they balance the look of the design.

6 Arrange the purple figs on top of the ingredients at different angles to complete the design. Check for any gaps and fill them with any remaining flower heads or a small trimmed broccoli floret.

Rest the bulbs at different angles to expose their textural roots and highlight their papery, semi-translucent skins.

Sunflowers in a wood vase

flower

Sunflower →

Rustic and quirky, this design is reminiscent of a beach boardwalk bathed in sunshine. Simply customize a jar by covering it in sticks of kindling wood and add sunflowers.

how to arrange

you will need

7 sunflowers

materials

Florist's scissors
Green tack
1 bag of kindling wood
1 clean recycled glass jar, just shorter
   than the lengths of kindling
Garden string, coloured string, or natural
   or coloured raffia

1 Fix 2 horizontal strips of green tack at equal distances around the jar. Stick the lengths of kindling onto the green tack in straight vertical lines, butting them up against each other.

2 Wind string around the wood and tie in a knot. Half-fill the jar with water. Add the sunflowers, trimming their stems so they sit just above the rim of wood. Top up with more water.

 insider tips

• Remove all the leaves and cut and split the stems before arranging the sunflowers in the vase.

• The kindling used here is store-bought and so of a standard length. If you use other kindling, trim it with secateurs or a small hand saw if it is too long.

Zinnias in tea glasses

There are no real rules for making this captivating design of richly coloured zinnias in jewel-like Moroccan tea glasses. Use your judgement as to how best to place the glasses and how short to trim the flower stems. Zinnias only last for a day or two, so this is a fleeting display.

how to arrange

1 If you want to incorporate tea lights into the design, half-fill all but 3 of the tea glasses with water; otherwise, add water to all the tea glasses. Arrange the glasses along the length of a table or on a couple of shelves.

2 Trim the flower stems so that some flowers sit just above the rim of the tea glasses and others are taller. Place the flowers in the glasses, adding single blooms to some and no more than 3 or 4 flowers to others.

3 If you are using tea lights, add them to the empty tea glasses. Only light the tea lights while you are in the room, and make sure no flowers sit too close to, or overhang, the naked flames.

 *insider tips*

• Zinnias have a lot of foliage on their stems, so strip all the foliage off as soon as possible after buying the flowers and before conditioning them in water (p24); foliage drinks up water quickly and the flowers don't last long, so this helps to prolong their life slightly.

• Take care when stripping off the foliage: zinnias have fragile stems that can snap in half very easily.

flowers

Orange zinnia ↓   ← Red zinnia

Peach zinnia ↓

↑ Pink zinnia

Yellow zinnia →

you will need

7 red zinnias
4 orange zinnias
4 pink zinnias
4 peach zinnias
2 yellow zinnias

materials

Florist's scissors
12–14 Moroccan tea glasses
3 tea lights (optional)

Meadow flowers

This loose assembly of country flowers and grasses is as simple as it gets, although the ingredients are all carefully chosen to give a wonderful vision of a summer meadow. Place on a hall, kitchen, or outdoor table, or on a large coffee table, for the best effect.

how to arrange

1 Divide the ingredients into separate piles so you can see each variety clearly. Half-fill the jug with water.

2 Arrange the ingredients like a hand tie: hold 1 cornflower stem in your hand and add 1 cow parsley stem, a stem or 2 of lavender, and a small group of the grasses to it; adding the grasses in this way will create more of a statement. Add more of each variety in turn, twisting the bunch around slightly in the same direction before adding the next ingredient, so the flowers and grasses are equally distributed. Reserve a few stems of lavender if you are using the small ceramic jug.

3 Trim the stems so they are all roughly the same length, and drop the bunch into the jug so the stems flare out naturally and rather haphazardly. Top up the jug with water. If you want to incorporate the smaller jug into the design, trim the lavender stems quite short, fill the jug with water, and drop the stems into the jug, leaving them arranged quite haphazardly.

insider tips

• If you re-cut the stems and change the water every day, the arrangement should last for three to five days.

• Cornflowers often have buds on long stems; cut these stems off the main flower stem and add the buds to the design once arranged in the jug.

flowers and foliage

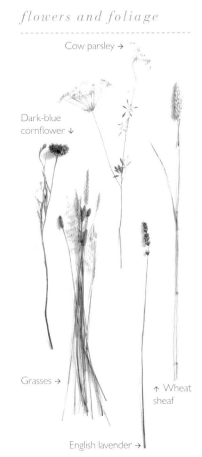

Cow parsley →

Dark-blue cornflower ↓

Grasses →

↑ Wheat sheaf

English lavender →

you will need

22 dark-blue cornflowers
25 English lavender
10 wheat sheafs
30 stems of various grasses
6 cow parsley

materials

White ceramic jug
Smaller white ceramic jug (optional)
Florist's scissors

Summertime scene

A few loosely arranged ingredients – wheat sheafs, green grasses, purple lavender, white cow parsley, and vibrant blue cornflowers – are all that is needed to give an evocative image of the countryside in summer.

Seasonal wreath

Making a wreath to use in every season is a wonderful way of decorating your door or mantelpiece throughout the year. The base of birch twigs will last indefinitely; just refresh the moss and replace the ivy and potted plants with new ingredients every two weeks or so.

flowers and foliage

Birch twig →

Trailing ivy ↓

Potted miniature kalanchoe ↓

Carpet moss →

signature details

After binding birch twigs and moss into place to make up the basic round shape of this wreath, you can keep the look quite simple or add a wealth of detail. This design evokes the onset of autumn, with the brilliant red petals of the kalanchoes set off by the more subdued hues of green and brown. Other natural material in the form of seagrass cord, which is wound around the birch twigs and moss to help define the round shape of the wreath, adds a small textural detail and more subtle colour.

you will need

2 large bunches birch twigs
Carpet moss
2 potted miniature kalanchoe plants (to fit inside the metal buckets)
3 strands trailing ivy

materials

Roll of thin reel wire
1 round wire frame 30cm (12in) in diameter
Seagrass cord
Florist's scissors
Secateurs (optional)
2 miniature galvanized metal buckets
Reel wire

for step by step, see overleaf →

Seasonal wreath
step by step

Insert the second bunch of twigs into the frame at the point where the loose twig ends from the first bunch start to branch out.

Tuck extra pieces of moss into the bound twigs around the outside of the round frame to give the wreath a three-dimensional look.

1 Cut the birch twigs down into 6 small bunches 20cm (8in) long. Tie them at their bases with wire. Fix 1 bunch onto the frame with wire. Add a second bunch in the same way.

2 As you add more bunches, insert moss in the gaps between the twigs and wire frame around the inside of the ring. Curve some loose twig ends around the metal ring and fix them to the frame with wire.

3 Add the remaining birch bunches and moss in the same way, until the wire frame is completely concealed and you have a solid base on which to build the seasonal elements.

Wind a length of wire around the metal frame and the lower half of the bunch of birch twigs to secure it in place.

Secure the moss and some of the loose birch twig ends in place, with wire wrapped around the circumference of the frame.

insider tips

• Stand the kalanchoe in their pots in a few centimetres of water, and the trails of ivy in a bucket of water, to give them a long drink before arranging them.

• Other ingredients to plant in the galvanized buckets through the year are spring bulbs, miniature rose plants, and miniature herbs.

Fix the wire in place by twisting the wire lengths tightly together against the side of the bucket and leaving two long loose ends.

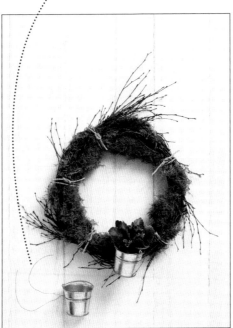

4 Cut 5 lengths of seagrass cord, each about 30cm (12in) long. Wrap each length twice around the circumference of the wreath, tie in a knot, and trim the ends. Repeat with the remaining lengths of cord, spacing them equally around the wreath.

5 Cut a long length of wire and wrap the centre of the wire around the bucket. Wrap the loose ends of the wire around the circumference of the frame so the pot hangs down from the wreath at a slight angle. Put the kalanchoe inside the bucket. Repeat with the second plant and bucket.

6 Add the trailing ivy, weaving each strand around the circumference of the wreath and tucking the leaves in between the loose twig ends. Trim off any twig ends that poke out too far, but keep the look quite loose and natural rather than manicured.

Cherry blossom bottles

Stylish and minimalist, yet full of interest and delicate charm, this simple asymmetrical design of white cherry blossom in old and recycled sprayed glass bottles perfectly captures the fresh new beauty of spring. Alter the scale completely according to where you place the arrangement.

how to arrange

1 To spray a glass bottle using a spray can, turn a cardboard box with a firm base onto its side in a well-ventilated room, or outside. Place the bottle inside the upturned box, cover your mouth and nose with a mask, and spray one side for 10 seconds only. Spray gently to avoid drips. Repeat, rotating the bottle in the same direction until the whole surface is sprayed and the colour has built up to your satisfaction. Allow to dry. Repeat with the remaining bottles.

2 Arrange the bottles in position – on the floor of a living room or dining room if you want a large-scale arrangement or on a table, shelf, mantelpiece, or dressing table for a smaller design – and fill some of the bottles with water.

3 Trim the blossom branches to different heights and cut and split each branch with secateurs, as they are woody and need help to drink up water. Place 1 stem in each water-filled vase. Use longer blossom branches for larger bottles and short stems for small bottles. Replace the water every two days.

insider tips

• Spray the bottles white, silver, or grey to retain a minimalist look.

• Don't overcrowd the number of bottles or the number of stems in a bottle – stick to 1 stem per bottle, or none if the arrangement benefits from it.

• Choose wine bottles, perfume bottles, or old bottles with texture or an interesting shape, but ensure that they are made of glass.

flower

← White cherry blossom

you will need

5 white cherry blossom branches (2 tall branches and 3 small branches)

materials

Large cardboard box
Spray mask
Spray cans of white, grey, and silver paint
Secateurs

substitutions

Magnolia branches in bud
Pink cherry blossom in neon-pink sprayed bottles

Juicy germinis

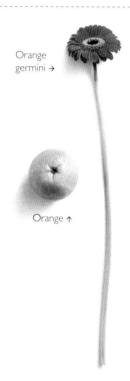

Orange
germini →

Orange ↑

Simple, yet unusual and amusing, oranges make excellent receptacles for germinis. An unexpected benefit is that the juice of the orange keeps the germini fresh all evening.

how to arrange

1 Cut the bottom of an orange with a knife to make a flat base. Push a closed pair of small scissors into the top to make a small, deep hole.

2 Trim the germini stem and push it into the hole so that it stands upright in the orange. Repeat with the rest of the germinis and oranges.

9 orange germinis (mini gerbera)
14 oranges
5 tea lights

Craft knife
Florist's scissors
Small scissors

 insider tips

• Give the germinis a long drink in deep water before arranging them in the fruit.

• In the remaining oranges, cut wider, shallower holes that will fit the size of a tea light. Insert a tea light into each hole so it sits flush with the rim of the orange.

Floral vintage tea set

Pick some small, delicate blooms from your garden and arrange them loosely in an old teapot and teacup for a delightfully simple, inexpensive, yet stylish arrangement on your coffee table or afternoon tea table. Choose only flowers that match the coloured pattern of your china.

flowers

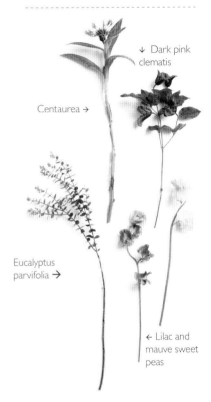

↓ Dark pink clematis

Centaurea →

Eucalyptus parvifolia →

← Lilac and mauve sweet peas

how to arrange

1 Half-fill the teapot with water. Hold the stem of each flower against the teapot to gauge the right length of stem and trim it before arranging it. Start with the clematis, as it is the biggest flower head: rest 4 clematis, evenly spaced, against the rim of the teapot and fill the gaps in between with a few sweet peas. Move in towards the middle of the arrangement, filling the neck of the teapot with more sweet peas and 3 of the centaureas. Check the blooms are evenly distributed.

2 Trim the eucalyptus down to 12 short stems, each about 4cm (1½in) long. Insert 6–7 stems at intervals around the edge of the pot and into any gaps in the centre.

3 For the teacup, informally arrange the remaining flowers and eucalyptus in your hand and tie the bunch at the base of the short stems using twine or string before placing it in the cup. Hand-tying the bunch in this way helps the flowers to flare out naturally, creating a pretty domed effect, and prevents the heavier flower heads from tipping out of the cup. Add water to the teacup and top up the teapot.

insider tips

• Although the sweet peas won't last long – at most, four days – change the water after two days to prolong their life.

• Place just one variety of flower in each container for a change, or to recreate this design en masse, arrange more flowers in a line of teacups or white mugs.

you will need

6 small dark-pink clematis
12 lilac and mauve sweet peas
7 centaureas
3 eucalyptus parvifolia stems

materials

1 vintage teapot, 1 teacup and saucer
Florist's scissors
Garden string or twine

substitution

Tulips in similar colours for a more modern look

Lilac petals and pussy willow

flowers and foliage

← Pussy willow

↓ Lilac
hydrangea

Lilac ↑
sweet pea

you will need

10–15 lilac sweet peas
1 lilac hydrangea
1 bunch pussy willow stems

materials

3 clean recycled cans with
    labels removed
Florist's scissors
Secateurs (optional)

This simple design is all about hidden and revealed stems: of bountiful delicate lilac flower petals overflowing their cans alongside regimented, upright pussy willow stems.

how to arrange

1 Half-fill the cans with water. Cut the hydrangea stem short enough for the base of the flower head to rest on the rim of the can. Repeat with the sweet peas so their stems are hidden.

2 Trim the pussy willow to the same length; aim to create a pleasing sense of height in proportion to the flowers. The more stems you add, the more upright the arrangement.

 insider tips

• In order not to waste the pussy willow, cut the stems down first. Choose a bud about one third of the way down the stem and, using secateurs, cut the stem at an angle just above the bud. Make a second cut two-thirds of the way down. Repeat with the other stems.

• Strip off pussy willow buds that will sit below the waterline, so they don't turn mouldy in the water.

Lilac sweet peas

The filmy pastel-coloured petals of these delicate sweet peas, which twist and unfurl as they open, releasing a beautiful fragrance, are a perfect example of "less is more" – one of our fundamental principles.

Asclepias eggcups

A fun table arrangement like this is perfect for an Easter-morning breakfast or a children's Easter party. These bright flowers have all been chosen to resemble the yellow and orange yolks of birds' eggs, and are small enough to create a dainty but lively eye-catching design.

how to arrange

1 Place the 3 eggshell bases in eggcups and fill the shells with water. Fill the rest of the eggcups with water and arrange them all in the centre of a kitchen or dining room table. If you want to use the tops of the eggshells, arrange them upside down on the table among the eggcups, and pour a little water into each.

2 Trim the flower stems very short, so the flowers peep out from the eggcups. Restrict the design to just 1 variety of flower per eggcup. Some varieties, like freesia and craspedia, look best with just 1 or 2 stems in each eggcup. Others, like matricaria and asclepias, have small clusters of flowers at the end of each stem and generally look better arranged en masse.

3 Fill every eggcup and any upturned shells with flowers. To add more detail to the design, cut off the stems from any odd leftover flowers and arrange the delicate flower heads on the table in between the eggcups.

 *insider tips*

• Choose flowers that resemble the colour of a yellow or orange egg yolk.

• As the eggshells and eggcups hold so little water, it is important to condition and stand the flowers in fresh water for about an hour before arranging them. Keep checking the water levels once you have arranged the flowers; they will drink up the available water quickly.

flowers

← Yellow freesia

Yellow matricaria ↓

← Yellow craspedia

Orange asclepias →

you will need

3 craspedia
5 yellow freesia
6 orange asclepias
3 matricaria

materials

3 eggshells
10–14 white ceramic eggcups
Florist's scissors

Mixed flowers in jam jars

Showing off flowers in a simple, low-key way in separate containers captures the detail and delight of every bloom. Use as many or as few jars as you like for this adaptable, easy arrangement, adding mixtures of short-stemmed garden blooms in a random but pleasing way.

how to arrange

1 For each jar, trim the stems of 4–5 mixed blooms, or a single variety of flower, making sure that the height of the flowers are not more than twice the height of the jar, and preferably shorter.

2 Half-fill a jar with water and add ¼ sterilizing tablet. Arrange the flowers loosely in the jar; there is no need to spiral the stems or tie the bunch together. Repeat with the rest of the flowers and jars.

3 Tie a matching ribbon around a few of the jars if you would like to give them more of a celebratory feel. Arrange the jars on a couple of shelves, in a line along a table, or place one in front of each place setting at a dining table. The flowers will last for up to five days if you trim their stems and refresh the water.

 *insider tips*

• If you don't own a garden, or can't find this particular selection of flowers, choose varieties with medium and small flower heads in a harmonious range of colours (p13).

• For a more rustic look, use raffia or coloured string instead of ribbon.

flowers

← Blue delphinium
↓ Astrantia
↓ Bouvardia
↓ Sweet William
Pink spray ↓ rose
← Veronica
↑ Flowering marjoram
← Dark-pink dahlia
← Forget-me-not

you will need

4 veronica
6 blue delphiniums
12 sweet Williams
16 forget-me-not
5 dark-pink dahlia
4 astrantia
7 flowering marjoram
4 bouvardia
4 pink spray roses

materials

Up to 10 clean glass jam jars
Florist's scissors
Coloured ribbon (optional)
Sterilizing tablets

Leather leaf fern in bottles

The key to this modern take on Victorian botany, with its specimen-like bottles displaying stems of leather leaf, lies in choosing recycled bottles with a hint of colour. Leather leaf is a great long-lasting foliage, but has an old-fashioned image. This design gives it a new lease of life.

how to arrange

1 Place the bottles or jars in position and half-fill a few with water. Fill the largest bottle or jar with 10cm (4in) of water and add a sterilizing tablet. Add ½ sterilizing tablet to each of the small jars.

2 Trim the largest fern stem, place the end of the stem in the base of the biggest jar, and curl and spiral the stem inside the jar so the fern fronds sit attractively behind the glass without looking squashed or unbalanced. Add a second stem in the same way, curling it in the same direction as you arrange it.

3 Trim the smaller stems of fern and arrange them in the remaining water-filled jars and bottles to create an asymmetrical design that shows off the delicate fern fronds. Add any foraged finds, such as feathers, to the empty bottles.

insider tips

• For the best composition, choose a variety of fern sizes and place no more than 1 or 2 stems in each bottle or jar.

• The leather leaf fern should last about one month. Only change the water when it looks murky (which will probably be about once a week).

• If you are entertaining, lift one of the bottles from the grouped arrangement to sit temporarily in a fireplace, on a guest bedside table, or on a dinner table for an evening meal.

foliage

← leather leaf fern fronds

you will need

2 or more leather leaf fern fronds

materials

Florist's scissors
Sterilizing tablets
Recycled jars and bottles in various sizes and shapes
Foraged finds

Hanging flowers

A loose, freestyle design of small mixed blooms in a home-made hanging jar can provide an unexpectedly delightful decorative detail to lift the appearance of any doorway, room, or garden. Use a mix of just a few garden and bought flowers for a truly eclectic arrangement.

how to arrange

1 First, make the handle for the jar. Holding the end of a 50cm (20in) length of wire against one side of the jar, bend the wire over the top of the jar and hold the other end in place on the other side of the glass. To fix the handle in place, tightly wind another, longer, length of wire about 6 times around the rim of the jar and over each side of the wire handle, leaving a short length of wire free at either end of the handle. Twist one of these short loose handle ends around one end of the longer wire, and repeat on the other side. Trim off any loose wire. Check that the handle is secure and the wire won't unravel.

2 Half-fill the jar with water and add ½ sterilizing tablet. Trim the stems of the camomile and arrange them in the jar so the flowers create a slight domed shape beneath the handle. Add the astrantia and freesia, trimming their stems to similar lengths and tucking them in between the camomile.

3 Add the veronica and flowering mint, letting their tall flower heads sit slightly above the other blooms. Cut the individual rose heads from their main stem. Tuck them into the centre of the arrangement and around the neck of the jar to create a small cluster of bright-pink blooms. Trim the stems of the sweet Williams and place them in any obvious gaps. Ensure that all the stems are in water, topping up with more water if necessary. Then hang up the jar by its handle.

 *insider tip*

• To create more impact, make up more jars in different sizes with handles, add just a tea light to some jars, and intersperse them with the hanging designs.

flowers

Freesia ↓
Camomile ↓
Veronica ↓
Flowering mint ↓
← Astrantia
← Sweet William
← Spray rose

you will need

2 veronica
1 flowering mint
2 freesias
2 sweet Williams
1 pink spray rose
2 camomile
1 astrantia

materials

Clean glass jar
Medium-gauge decorative wire or craft wire
Pliers
Florist's scissors
½ sterilizing tablet

Wrapped rose bouquet

This is a stylish way to show off blooms without the need for added foliage, or to practise a simplified variation of a spiral stem technique if you want to give away a bouquet as a gift. The roses can be unwrapped or left as they are and transferred straight to a vase.

signature details

The joy of arranging this bouquet is that the individual rose flower heads are given sufficient definition, separation, and support by their tissue wrappings, which does away with the need for graduating the flower heads or using a proper spiral stem technique (pp36–37). They can simply be gently piled on top of one another at slight angles to imitate a hand tie and create the impression of a sophisticated layered, slightly rounded bouquet. The complementary colour of the lilac tissue paper enhances the peachy hues of the roses, so that they resonate more intensely with their packaging than without.

flower

Peach 'Miss Piggy' rose →

you will need

12 peach 'Miss Piggy' roses

materials

Florist's scissors
12 sheets lilac tissue paper
Lilac ribbon
Clear cellophane

substitutions

White roses in black tissue paper
Red peonies in green tissue paper
Red amaryllis in lime-green tissue paper

for step by step, see overleaf

Wrapped rose bouquet
step by step

Once wrapped, the rose should sit just above the crossed-over tissue paper, with the pointed corner right behind the flower head.

1 Strip all but a few small leaves from the stem of each rose. Fold a sheet of tissue paper in half lengthways on a flat surface and lay 1 rose at an angle across it, so the flower head rests on the top-right corner of the paper.

2 Fold the bottom right corner of the tissue paper over the rose stem, tucking it under the stem slightly. Pinch the folded tissue paper together halfway down the stem to keep it in place.

3 Roll the rose in the tissue paper, pinching the tissue at the same point as you roll. The rose head should sit just proud of the tissue. Repeat with the rest of the roses and tissue paper.

The point at which you pinch the tissue paper around the stem will become the binding point for the whole bouquet.

• Avoid handling the tissue paper too much as you roll up the roses and tie them together; the tissue should remain as crisp and smooth as possible.

• The roses should last for one week if you re-cut the stems and change the water every couple of days.

4 Arrange 4 of the wrapped roses on a flat surface with the stems lightly crossed over at the binding point. Add another rose so it sits just below the other flower heads.

5 Tie the bouquet at the binding point with a piece of ribbon and trim off the loose ends. This ribbon will be hidden by a larger ribbon tied in a bow, so its appearance doesn't matter.

Place more wrapped roses on top of the arranged pile, interspersing them around this core bunch so that every rose is visible.

6 Wrap a large length of cellophane around the bouquet, scrunching it up at the binding point. Cut a long length of ribbon and wind it around the binding point, finishing it off in a flamboyant bow.

'Miss Piggy' roses

The coral colour of these handsome single-headed roses can truly be appreciated close up: the furled petals at the centre, which are almost light orange in hue, graduate to large outer petals in shades of warm pink.

Vase arrangements

As well as showing you a classic approach to arranging flowers in a vase at the beginning of this chapter, we have also transformed a selection of ordinary vases into the inspiration for an exciting and dynamic range of flower designs, which all look dramatically different.

Rose and gloriosa sunburst

Designed as a front-facing, stand-alone piece for a buffet table or hall table, this glorious mix of tonal flowers and foliage is an organic design that evolves as you add and adjust the different stems. It should last for five days if you change the water after two days.

A front-facing arrangement has a unique three-dimensional shape, almost like a teardrop when viewed from the side, with shorter stems massing at the front and sides near the top of the vase, and a few longer stems at the back that frame the whole arrangement. Here, a selection of flowers in yellow and pinky-peach hues is framed by tall stems of green privet and red robin foliage, which adds extra texture and depth of colour.

flowers and foliage

Yellow gloriosa lily ↓   Red robin ↓

Yellow kangaroo paw ↓

← Privet

Orange → snapdragon

Yellow ↑ rose   ↑ Cream double lisianthus

you will need

8 yellow roses
5 cream double lisianthus
5 yellow kangaroo paw
3 yellow gloriosa lily
5 orange snapdragons
4–5 privet stems
4–5 red robin (photinia) stems

materials

Florist's scissors
1 large cylindrical glass vase
  approximately 30cm (12in) high
Sterilizing tablet

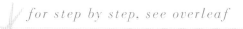

for step by step, see overleaf

Rose and gloriosa sunburst
step by step

Create height with 1 tall foliage stem and angle other stems forwards, upwards, and outwards to create an oval shape.

1 Half-fill the vase with water and add a sterilizing tablet. Create a framework for the arrangement with a three-dimensional effect using the red robin and privet foliage.

2 Add the snapdragons, matching the height and width of the foliage, but keeping them within the confines of the foliage leaves. This colour helps to build the background framework.

3 Add the gloriosa lilies. Always put delicate flowers such as these around the edges of the arrangement, as they add a softer, more refined edge to the design.

Strip all the leaves from the lower stems of the flowers and foliage. All the stems inside the vase should cross at a central point.

insider tip

• The shortest stems should be more acutely angled, and arranged at the base of the design near the rim of the vase for the best three-dimensional effect.

• Keep a sense of air and space in the finished design, especially around the edges.

Keep tall stems of lisianthus for the back of the design in the centre and cut down stems for the front and sides of the arrangement.

The tips of the lisianthus stems are very delicate, so be careful that you don't knock off their heads as you add other flowers.

4 Add the lisianthus. Insert the shorter stems at an angle to fill out the sides, following the diagonal line of the snapdragons.

5 Add the kangaroo paw, keeping the stems long and inserting them into the gaps between the other blooms. You should now have a strong three-dimensional shape of mixed flowers and foliage.

6 Roses are visually quite dense and solid, so they work better when arranged together as a cluster towards the centre of the display rather than distributed individually around the edges.

To maintain the height and proportions of the design, restrict the tallest stems for the centre back of the arrangement.

Mixing texture and colour

Interesting flower shapes and textures predominate in
this mix of ingredients. The colour scheme – bright,
saturated yellow combined with soft hues of pink, peach,
and orange – helps to heighten the textural detail.

Rosemary hedge

foliage

Rosemary →

Dense enough to give the illusion of a hedge, easy to trim into a uniform shape, and with a delicious fragrance, rosemary is the ideal foliage for a stylish topiary design.

how to arrange

you will need

5 large bunches of rosemary with
approximately 20 stems in each bunch

materials

Florist's scissors
5 glass cube vases 10x10cm (4x4in)
Sterilizing tablets
4 small glass cube vases 8x8cm (3x3in)
(optional; see tips)
4 floating candles (optional; see tips)

1 Arrange the rosemary so the stems are parallel and their tips are level. Trim the stems to 30cm (12in) long. Half-fill a cube vase with water and add ½ sterilizing tablet.

2 Put the cut stems in the vase. Add more stems if they do not stand upright. Repeat with the rest of the rosemary and vases. Trim the tips, if needed, to give the hedge a flat top.

 insider tips

• Pour the same amount of water into 4 small cube vases and place a floating candle in each vase. Arrange the small vases in between the larger vases.

• Replace the water every other day; woody stems quickly turn water muddy.

• When you break up the design, hang some rosemary under your shower head; the hot water releases the oils in the leaves to fragrance the room.

Flowers with seashells

These flowers and foliage have been chosen to recreate a seaside garden. Like most coastal plants that withstand drying sea winds, they have small flowers and leaf surfaces to conserve moisture. They last for one week if you re-cut individual stems and refresh the water.

signature details

This asymmetrical all-round arrangement looks different from every angle, with some stems left longer than others to create a natural, loose, very informal display rather than a tightly regulated design. Plenty of texture and visual interest is provided by the seashell casing and the differently shaped flowers and foliage in their soft pastel shades; the unusual allium 'Schubertii', with its long, tendril-like stems, is specially chosen for its resemblance to an underwater sea anemone.

flowers and foliage

Allium 'Schubertii' →

'Sharon' fern →

Stachys →

Foxtail →

White wax flower →

you will need

2 allium 'Schubertii'
2 white wax flowers
6 'Sharon' fern stems
4 foxtails
6 stachys

materials

1 clear glass column vase 20x20cm (8x8in)
1 vase 15x12cm (6x5in)
Chicken wire
Small seashells
Sterilizing tablet

for step by step, see overleaf

Flowers with seashells
step by step

Gently mould the chicken wire into a loose ball, so its holes are large enough to hold several stems once in place inside the vase.

Cover the small vase with an extra piece of cellophane or paper while adding seashells if you want to prevent any dropping into it.

1 Place a layer of shells in the bottom of the large vase and even it out so it is level. Stand the small vase on the shells and insert moulded chicken wire into it. Half-fill it with water to weigh it down and add a sterilizing tablet.

2 Fill the gap created between the walls of the 2 vases with more seashells. Trim the 2 alliums. Rest the stem of 1 allium against the rim of the vase and insert the other into the chicken-wire ball on the opposite side of the vase.

3 Trim the stems of the 4 foxtails to slightly different lengths and insert 3 into the chicken wire on one side of the vase. Place the fourth foxtail on the opposite side of the vase.

• Although you won't see the water that the stems sit in, add a sterilizing tablet anyway: it will help to mask the slight onion odour that alliums give off.

• If you can't find allium 'Schubertii', or the flowers are out of season, chrysanthemums would make a good substitute.

Stachys is pale and soft in texture and would get lost if it is distributed individually around the design, so concentrate it in one area.

4 Trim the ferns to various lengths. Stand some ferns upright in the chicken-wire frame and angle others out to the sides to create an asymmetrical effect.

5 Cut down the long stems of white wax flower into shorter stems and insert them in between the other stems to fill any obvious gaps. Wax flowers are tiny, so add groups of 2 or 3 stems at a time if you don't want them to look bitty.

6 Add the stems of stachys in a cluster at the front or centre of the arrangement. Then top up the smaller inner vase with water.

Calla lily and dogwood bowl

The graceful curving heads of calla lilies can be shown off to perfection in a circular fish bowl, with the minimum of ingredients required to complete the look. Green dogwood is the exact colour of calla lily stems and, here, it is arranged to look almost like an extension of the flower stems.

how to arrange

1 Cut the thicker end off the bottom of each dogwood stem to leave about 80cm (32in) of thinner, more pliable stem. Trim off all the small side shoots to give each stem a smooth, streamlined look.

2 Fill the fish bowl with 5–6cm (2–2½in) of water and add a sterilizing tablet.

3 Arrange the dogwood stems first. Insert the base of each stem into the water, and curve and twist the stem into place inside the rounded bowl so it rises up and down in a circular swirl. Repeat with the rest of the dogwood to create a balanced sculptural framework that will help to support the calla lily flower heads.

4 Hold a calla lily so its head points towards you. Gently massage the stem from tip to base with your thumb and forefinger (p26). This will break the fibres in the stem, allowing it to bend (if you massage too firmly, you will crush the stem). The head will droop as you massage the stem. Repeat with the rest of the calla lilies.

5 Gently bend a flower stem into place in the bowl, ensuring that the base of the stem sits in water and the flower head is supported by the dogwood framework. Arrange the rest of the calla lilies evenly around the bowl at different heights, and make sure they don't sit too close to each other. You can point all the lilies in the same direction, but it's not essential.

insider tips

• Use very fresh dogwood so that it will bend easily.

• Use young flowers; older lilies cannot easily be massaged and may fall apart.

flower and foliage

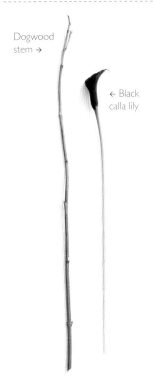

Dogwood stem →

← Black calla lily

you will need

6 dogwood stems
10 black calla lilies

materials

1 clear glass fish bowl vase
   (25.5cm/10in high)
Sterilizing tablet
Secateurs

substitutions

White and purple 'Vermeer' calla lilies
Tulips

Compact spring bouquet

Arranging delicate bright bluebells, alchemilla, and foliage in a spiral hand tie keeps this design as neat as possible in its customized jar. Many stems in a small vase drink up water quickly, but if you refresh the water every other day and trim the stems, the display lasts for a week.

signature details

A spiral stem arrangement gives this delightful small bouquet of pretty spring flowers and foliage a domed shape that looks good from every angle. The display is lifted to another level of decorative detail and interest with the unusual vase, which is simply an empty jam jar covered in lengths of snakegrass and tied with seagrass cord. Place this design in a study, a bathroom, or on a bedside table for the best effect.

flowers

Alchemilla mollis →
Bluebell ↓
↓ Senecio
← Hebe
↑ Snakegrass stem
↑ Eucalyptus parvifolia

you will need

Approximately 20 snakegrass stems
10 bluebells
4 senecio stems
2 eucalyptus parvifolia stems
5 hebe stems
6 alchemilla mollis

materials

1 clean empty jam jar
Florist's scissors
Green tack
Seagrass cord
Garden string, twine, or raffia

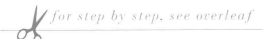

for step by step, see overleaf

Compact spring bouquet
step by step

It doesn't matter at this stage if you cut the stems into uneven lengths, as long as each stem is longer than the height of the jar.

Wind a long length of seagrass cord several times around the snakegrass stems near the base of the jar.

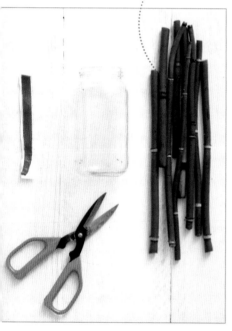

1 Cut the lengths of snakegrass in half with scissors or secateurs. Cover the sides of the jam jar with 2 horizontal strips of green tack.

2 Stick the snakegrass stems onto the jar in very straight vertical lines, butting them right up against one another to completely conceal the clear glass.

3 Cover the whole jar with stems of snakegrass, then tie a length of seagrass cord around the stems and secure it firmly in a knot. Trim the ends of the knot to make it look neat.

insider tip

• If some of the flowers begin to fade, cut them out and add more small stems around the edges of the vase. Thread a few flowers into the centre of the bouquet too, if needed, to conceal any obvious gaps.

If the jar is very short, leave the snakegrass slightly longer at the top so its rim sits a little higher than that of the jar.

4 Trim the snakegrass stems straight across with scissors, at either end of the jar, so both the base and the rim look as even as possible.

5 Arrange the flowers and foliage as a spiral hand-tied bouquet (pp36–37), distributing the different ingredients evenly throughout the bunch. Secure the bunch with a length of string tied in a knot.

6 Half-fill the vase with water and add the bouquet, making sure all its stems are in water inside the jam jar. Move the vase into position and top up the jar with more water to just below the brim.

Check the height of the bouquet against the side of the vase and trim the stems so it sits just above the rim of the snakegrass vase.

Alstroemeria lollipops

Typically, alstroemeria look a little unexciting in a mixed arrangement, but a monochrome design maximizes their potential. Choose bright hues so the flowers almost pop in a fabulously vibrant, intense burst of colour against the complementary hues of their green leaves and stems.

← Orange
alstroemeria

← Deep pink
alstroemeria

how to arrange

1 Strip the long stems of their leaves, which tend to wither, especially just below the base of the flower. Take one stem and place your hand 5–6cm (2–2½in) below the flower head; this will be the binding point, which must be high up on the stem.
2 Add the remaining flowers – all the same colour – one at a time, inserting each into the bunch at a slight angle at the point where your thumb rests, so the end of the stem points towards you and the flower points away. Turn the bunch in the same direction after you add each stem to create a slight spiral effect (pp36–37).
3 Tie the bunch at the binding point with a length of seagrass tied in a simple knot. Use translucent nylon thread to tie the base of the stems together.
4 Pour 15cm (6in) of water into the tall glass vase, add a sterilizing tablet, and arrange the flowers at an angle. Trim the stems of one bunch so these flowers sit slightly lower in the vase.

 insider tips

• Leave the flower stems as long as possible if you want the arrangement to look like a giant lollipop. You can adjust the scale completely by using fewer flowers and trimming the stems so they are much shorter.

• Use matching coloured ribbon instead of seagrass to brighten the look further.

• Make up three arrangements and position them in a row in three identical vases for a dramatic floor or stair display.

you will need

15 orange alstroemeria
15 deep pink alstroemeria

materials

Seagrass cord
Translucent nylon thread
Florist's scissors
1 tall clear glass column or slightly
   flared vase
Sterilizing tablet

Pink alstroemeria

Arranging often ordinary-looking flowers close together
en masse can give beautiful and unexpected results.
Here, veins of dark pink running the length of each petal
become an interesting feature that adds depth and detail.

Bouvardia cube

This bright, modern geometric design is inspired by the "slices" of colour that run through seaside rock candy; we picked out two coloured gravels and matched the hues of the flowers to them. This design also looks striking if made up as a pair. It will last for five to seven days.

signature details

The simplicity of this design lies in the fact that it is restricted to just one variety of flower, but visual interest is created by choosing two saturated hues of bouvardia and making them up in individual bunches to create four squares of lively colour within one large slightly domed bouquet. A cube vase repeats the squared theme, while the gravel around the flowers sits in layers, like strata or seams, enhancing the geometric design and adding to the very textural look of this display.

flowers

Pink bouvardia →

Red bouvardia ↓

you will need

10 red bouvardias
10 pink bouvardias

materials

1 clear glass cube vase 12x12cm (5x5in)
1 glass cube vase 16x16cm (6x6in)
Florist's scissors
1 pot of pink gravel
1 pot of red gravel
Spoon (optional)
Funnel or sheet of A4 paper (optional)
Garden string

substitution

Roses in harmonious colours

for step by step, see overleaf

Bouvardia cube
step by step

The layer of red gravel must be thick enough for the rim of the small vase to sit at exactly the same height as the rim of the large vase.

Pour the gravel into the gap created between the vases. Try to keep the layers of gravel a similar depth to achieve uniformity.

1 Arrange a level layer of red gravel over the base of the large vase. Place the small vase on the gravel. If you like, use a funnel, or a sheet of A4 paper curled into a funnel shape, to pour more red gravel into the gap between the vases. Then add a thick layer of pink gravel.

2 Repeat with a final layer of red gravel to fill the gap between the vases, so the smaller vase is completely hidden behind the coloured layers of gravel. Half-fill the small vase with water.

Use the end of a spoon handle to adjust the gravel to ensure the top of each layer forms a straight, even line.

3 Strip all the large leaves from the flower stems and trim the stems to about 15cm (6in), so they are short enough to be arranged easily into bunches. (Once arranged, the stems will be cut again to exactly the right length to fit in the vase.)

insider tips

• The more leaves you remove from the bouvardia stems, the more water the flowers can drink up and the longer they will last.

• Re-cut the stems and refresh the water after two days to prolong the life of the flowers.

Some bouvardia flower heads are bigger than others, so adapt the number of stems, if needed, to create 4 evenly sized bunches.

Arrange the bunches using a spiral stem technique for a domed effect. Nudge the bunches into place to create a square shape.

4 Separate the flowers into 4 piles: 2 pink and 2 red, with 4–5 stems in each. Arrange the flowers using a spiral stem technique (pp36–37) and a medium binding point. Secure each bunch at the binding point using garden string tied in a knot.

5 Arrange the bunches as one bouquet, with the 2 pink and 2 red bunches positioned diagonally opposite each other to create a square chequerboard effect. Tie off the bouquet at the binding point.

6 Hold the tied flowers against the side of the vase to check the length of their stems, and trim them accordingly. Place the flowers in the small vase and top it up with water.

A medium binding point will prevent any gaps between the bunches, but allow the flowers to flare out and conceal the small cube vase.

Tulips in rosemary

A chic, small design such as this looks good on any shelf or table. Use a thin, straight-sided glass vase to achieve the right look and choose vibrantly coloured frilly red parrot tulips to complement the deep rich green hues of the smooth rosemary leaves and their silvery undersides.

how to arrange

1 Hold a stem of rosemary on its side against the front of the vase and trim it so it is exactly the same width as the vase. Place it inside the front of the vase so its horizontal leaves will conceal the stems of upright rosemary.

2 Trim the remaining stems of rosemary and stand them behind the horizontal stem in an upright row against the front of the vase, butting them up against one another. Trim their tips so they are the same height as the vase.

3 Fold a length of cellophane into a roll that is the same width as the vase. This will provide a base for the tulip stems to sit on and push the rosemary stems up against the front of the vase. Press the roll into position along the bottom of the vase. The rosemary should sit quite securely in place; if not, add another roll.

4 Half-fill the vase with water. Hold 1 tulip against the back of the vase (where the cellophane roll can be seen) and gauge how long the stem should be once standing on the roll. Check that the tulip head will sit immediately above the rosemary hedge and the rim of the vase. Trim the stem and place the tulip in the vase behind the rosemary. Repeat with the rest of the tulips, arranging them in even rows about three tulips deep. The design will last for five days if you refresh the water every day.

 insider tips

• Slit the neck of each tulip just below the head with a craft knife (p26) before trimming the stem and arranging it. This is a difficult arrangement to disturb once finished, and slitting the stems helps to prevent the tulips growing too tall.

flower and foliage

Rosemary ›

Red parrot tulip →

you will need

20 red parrot tulips
2 large bunches of rosemary

materials

Clear cellophane
Florist's scissors
Slim upright glass vase about 16cm (6½in) high, 20cm (8in) wide and 6cm (2½in) deep

'Rococo' parrot tulips

The extraordinary distorted outer petals of these parrot tulips, which make them look so unique, was originally caused by a virus that was introduced in the 17th century during "Tulip mania", when tulips were coveted.

Dahlias and rose petals

This stunning table arrangement of flower petals displayed in different ways is deceptively easy. Six cube vases, each with four untied dahlias resting on their rims, are arranged in a precise line and interspersed with uniform trails of velvety red rose petals.

how to arrange

1 Line each cube vase with a horizontal green tie leaf curled into position to hide the stems of the dahlias. Fill each vase with water and add a sterilizing tablet.

2 Check the height of each dahlia stem against the side of the vase and cut it short enough for the flower head to rest on the rim of the container. Place 4 dahlias in each vase and adjust the flowers slightly so they both fill each corner and butt up against one another so no gaps are visible.

3 Hold the stem of a rose in one hand and pull off the flower head cleanly but gently with your other hand. Very gently unfurl the petals onto a plate or bowl.

4 Evenly space the vases along the length of the table. Arrange the rose petals in short lines in between them. Overlap the petals for added impact.

insider tips

• Unfurling rose petals onto a plate will help to catch the tiny stamens in the centre of the flower that could otherwise scatter over the table and spoil the clean look of the design. Don't handle the petals too much, as they bruise easily.

• The tiny petals around the base of a dahlia flower can quickly wither and curl up, so pull these off before arranging the flower.

• The dahlias will last for about four days but the rose petals will fade sooner, so break up the table arrangement once you have finished entertaining and distribute the dahlia vases around the house.

flowers and foliage

Red rose →

Pink dahlia →

Green tie leaf →

you will need

20 pink dahlias
3 red roses
6 green tie leaves

materials

6 clear glass cube vases 10x10cm (4x4in)
Florist's scissors
Sterilizing tablets

Deconstructed bouquet

Most budget bouquets are cheap, cheerful, and long-lasting, but they can also look garish and rather jumbled. This design maximizes the qualities of these mixed ingredients by separating, conditioning, and displaying them in clever ways to improve their appeal.

signature details

The benefit of a ready-made budget bouquet of flowers is that you can decorate your house with fun designs that are simple and speedy to arrange. The golden rule is to separate out the different varieties and colours and treat each as an individual arrangement. Here, carnations are given structure and form using a spiral stem technique, while yellow chrysanthemums are transformed into delicate flower heads with intricate green sepals and suspended inside a clear glass fish bowl vase.

flowers and foliage

Alstroemeria →
Spray ↓ chrysanthemum
Ruscus ↓
Solidago ↓
↑ Carnation
← Palm frond

you will need

1 ready-made bouquet of flowers, which typically includes:
4 stems of spray chrysanthemums (2 yellow, 1 pink, 1 white)
12 carnations (9 pale pink, 3 yellow)
1 alstroemeria
1 ruscus
1 solidago
1 palm frond

materials

Florist's scissors
Variety of glass vases, bottles, and glasses
Sterilizing tablets

for step by step, see overleaf

Deconstructed bouquet
step by step

Most budget bouquets will have had minimal attention, so it is important to condition both flowers and foliage before arranging them.

Chrysanthemum petals are quite hardy, so they will last well and not turn mushy once in contact with the water.

1 Divide the mixed bunch into separate varieties and colours to see what you have, and think about the best container for each. Then strip off excess leaves from the flowers and foliage, trim their stems, and stand them in a bucket of cool fresh water for 1 hour.

2 Chrysanthemum flowers are light, so they suit a floating arrangement. Half-fill a clear glass fish bowl with water. Cut off the stem immediately below each yellow flower head and float it on the water. Don't overcrowd the bowl; if you have lots of flowers, fill a second bowl.

3 Cut the short individual stems of pink and white chrysanthemum flowers from their main stems. Arrange the flowers loosely in separate wine or water glasses.

Spray chrysanthemums have many flowers on each stem and so can be difficult to arrange. These flowers look best arranged individually.

insider tip

• Add 1 sterilizing tablet to every large clear glass vase of water and ½ tablet to each small glass, bottle, or jar before adding the different flowers and foliage.

There is no need to tie the binding point with string, as the upright shape of the column vase will hold the spiralled stems in place.

Position the different arrangements together in a random design on a table or along a shelf, or distribute them around your home.

4 Carnations work well as a compact bunch. Use a high binding point, holding the stems just under the flower heads, and arrange them using a spiral technique (pp36–37). Drop the bunch into a small column vase half-filled with water.

5 Trim the stem of the alstroemeria and place it in a tall bottle or slim vase filled with water. Add a stem of ruscus if you have it and like the effect it gives, but keep the look minimalist to show off the long elegant flower stem and trumpet-like petals at the top.

6 Place the palm leaf frond in a small column vase of water and cut straight across the spiky tips that sit above the rim of the vase. Trim the stem of solidago and place it in a bottle half-filled with water.

Floral foam displays

The great benefit of floral foam is that it enables you to support flowers, in a way that you can't with a vase of water, to create interesting shapes and displays. Take care to soak the foam thoroughly before cutting it to fit the container exactly (squashed dry foam will not absorb water well), and you will achieve success with these imaginative designs.

Summer garden flowers

A classic approach to flower arranging is given a fresh twist in this slightly asymmetrical arrangement. It includes a mix of silvery green foliage that complements the harmonious hues of the flowers and gives added texture and visual interest.

signature details

The shape of this front-facing arrangement is deliberately designed so that the ingredients all face forwards or out to the sides, while the back of the display is flat, so it can be positioned against a wall on a sideboard or hall table, for example. An absence of strong dark green foliage in the arrangement gives it an informal, updated look and allows the harmonious colour palette of pastel pink, purple, lilac, grey, and silver shades to resonate together to give a soft, romantic feel.

flowers

← Purple sweet peas

Purple clematis ↓

Purple lisianthus ↓

Lilac spray roses ↓

← Trailing jasmine

Eucalyptus → parvifolia

↑ Rosemary

Senecio →

← Blue delphinium

you will need

5 eucalyptus parvifolia stems
7 senecio stems
2 bushy bunches of rosemary
6 purple lisianthus
10 purple sweet peas
6 purple clematis
11 blue delphiniums
10 lilac spray roses
3 trailing jasmine stems

materials

1 waterproof urn or shallow vase
Small floral foam blocks
Craft knife
Florist's scissors

for step by step, see overleaf

Summer garden flowers
step by step

Eucalyptus foliage has the longest stems and provides the best framework on which to build the fan shape of this design.

Check the height of each flower against the framework of foliage before you trim the end and insert it into the foam.

1 Soak small foam blocks (p161) and push them into the urn to make a raised base. Insert 1 stem of eucalyptus in the top and 2 at a downwards angle at either side.

2 Build up the basic shape with more, but not all, of the foliage evenly dispersed throughout the arrangement, and the shorter stems of rosemary inserted at the front. Reserve the remaining foliage.

3 Add some long, strong stems of lisianthus to the back and sides. Insert the stems at the sides at a downwards angle so the flowers point upwards. Repeat with the delphiniums.

The foam must sit proud of the urn so you can insert some stems at an upwards angle to give shape to the design and hide the urn rim.

Rosemary is a dense-looking foliage, so trim these stems quite short and add them to the centre of the design to give it weight.

insider tips

• When working with floral foam, make sure the flowers and foliage are cut and conditioned and left to stand in fresh water for at least an hour before arranging them.

• To get the right height, you will need flowers with long stems for this design, so look for long-stemmed sweet peas. The longest stems in this arrangement are approximately 55cm (21½in); reduce or increase the size of the arrangement according to your surroundings.

• Top up the container with water every day and mist the flowers so they last longer.

4 Add the sweet peas and clematis, angling the stems at the sides. Insert stems at the base of the foam at an upwards angle, so the flowers point down to hide the rim of the urn.

5 Add the roses, loosely massing the majority of blooms in the centre, and placing a few around the top and edges. Balance out the arrangement with any remaining flowers and check for any gaps.

6 Add the trailing jasmine to the front of the foam at one side. Strip off the leaves before you add it, as they tend to die quickly. It may need to be replaced after a few days.

Fill any obvious gaps in the design with individual stems of the reserved foliage, but don't overfill the arrangement.

The design is dense with clusters of roses and rosemary at the centre, and looser and more airy around the edges.

Harmonious highlights

The pink spray roses that dominate the centre of this arrangement are a large-headed variety, and are specially chosen to ensure they stand out in this harmonious arrangement of pinks, blues, and purples.

Sunflower topiary tree

Topiary trees are a great way of displaying large and small flowers and foliage in "close-up", so that every ingredient is clearly visible; together they create a wonderfully tactile design. Place on a hall table, or position a pair of topiary trees either side of a doorway.

signature details

Just like a real ornamental tree cut into shape, this design has a clearly defined form that dictates the arrangement of bright yellow and orange flowers, unripe berries, and dried, papery seed heads: every ingredient sits flush against the surface of a floral foam ball to create a circular all-round display. Natural details, such as a mound of carpet moss over the surface of the pot, make the birch pole look like a firmly planted tree trunk. The moss also hides the foam and trimmed cellophane.

for step by step, see overleaf →

flowers and foliage

Blackberry stem →

Orange spray rose ↓

Mini sunflower ↓

↑ Scabious seed head

Hebe →

you will need

5 hebe stems
10 mini sunflowers
10 orange spray roses
25 scabious seed heads
10 blackberry stems

materials

1 floral foam ball 16cm (6in) in diameter
Rectangle of floral foam
Craft knife
Florist's scissors
1 terracotta pot 16cm (6in) in diameter and 24cm (10in) tall
1 birch pole 45–50cm (18–20in) long
Hand saw
Cellophane or a bin liner

Sunflower topiary tree
step by step

Cut the hebe stems to 5cm (2in) and evenly space them around the ball so there are plenty of gaps in between each short stem.

Cut any large sprays of blackberries into 2 shorter sprays before trimming the stems and inserting them into the foam.

1 Line the pot with cellophane. Cut the foam roughly to fit the pot, then soak the foam and ball in water (p161). Trim the wet foam and push it into the pot. Press the pole into the foam so it stands upright, and press the ball onto the pole. Insert short stems of hebe foliage into the foam ball.

2 Trim the stems of the mini sunflowers to 5cm (2in) and insert them evenly around the ball, pressing them straight in towards the centre of the ball. Judge by eye how many flowers to insert.

3 Strip any large leaves from the unripe blackberries, trim the stems to 5cm (2in), and insert them into the florist's foam, distributing them evenly around the ball.

As you press the birch pole into the foam in the pot, take care not to puncture the waterproof cellophane lining.

• The foam may dry out quickly due to the large amount of flowers and foliage used in this design, so mist the arrangement daily.

• If you can't find a birch pole, try using five bamboo canes tied together.

If you can still see some foam after inserting the scabious seed heads, add a small stem of hebe or a single spray of blackberries.

4 Cut the spray roses into individual stems of 5cm (2in). Gather them into groups of 3 stems and insert them into some of the remaining gaps in the foam. Arranging them in this way creates an impact of shape and colour and avoids the design looking too bitty.

5 Trim the scabious seed heads and insert them into the foam. Hold the scabious by their stems rather than their heads, as they are very fragile.

6 Cut off the excess cellophane. Cover the surface of the pot with carpet moss shaped into a gentle mound to conceal the floral foam and trimmed cellophane.

There should now be just a few gaps in the foam. Fill these last gaps with the seed heads. Add them individually or in pairs.

Gypsophila wreath

flower

Pink →
gypsophila

An all-season wreath made up of delicate clusters of gypsophila becomes a gorgeous door or table decoration for a party, a christening, or a spring or outdoor celebration.

how to arrange

1 Immerse the ring in water (p161). Insert 3 gypsophila sprays into the inside of the ring at a downwards angle so they point out. Add more grouped sprays 1cm (½in) apart.

2 Insert stems on top straight down and those around the outside at a downwards angle. Angle the stems upwards at the outside edges of the ring so the flowers hide the base.

you will need

20–25 stems pink gypsophila

materials

1 floral foam ring with a base, 30cm (12in) in diameter
Florist's scissors
Strong thread or wire if you want to hang the wreath

substitution

White gypsophila against a dark wooden door for a wintery look

 insider tips

• Trim 5cm (2in) from the long gypsophila stems, stand them in deep water for an hour, and then cut off the many small sprays. Trim the short stems of these sprays to 1cm (½in) before arranging them.

• If you mist the wreath well once a day to keep the flowers fresh, it should last for a week.

Alliums in a trough

Long, straight stems of allium offset by horizontal lengths of bamboo, which conceal the workings of the arrangement and convey a hint of the Orient, make up this impressively precise, minimal display. This structural design looks fantastic in a modern space with clean lines.

how to arrange

1 Line the trough with cellophane if it is not watertight. Cut the foam to an approximate size to fit in the trough, then immerse it in a bucket or sink of water for about 3 minutes, until soaked and no more bubbles rise up (don't over-soak it). Push the foam into place; if there are any gaps, fill with more pieces of soaked foam.

2 Trim the allium stems, if needed, so they are all the same length. Insert an allium stem into either corner of the foam at the back of the trough. Insert 3 stems into the foam in between these 2 alliums, spacing them evenly to make a perfectly straight row of alliums.

3 Repeat the process by placing 1 allium in front of each arranged stem to create a middle row of alliums sitting in line.

4 Insert the last 5 alliums in the same way to form an identical front row.

5 Trim the bamboo into 6 equal lengths that are a little longer than the width of the trough. Cut each end on a diagonal using secateurs. Thread the bamboo in between the 3 rows of alliums, so they sit in straight horizontal lines and conceal the surface of the foam. The design should last for one week.

insider tips

• Part of the onion family, alliums give off a natural onion odour. To eliminate this smell, add ½ teaspoon of bleach to the water before you soak the foam.

• Drizzle water onto the florist's foam every other day, or more often, if the foam feels dry to the touch.

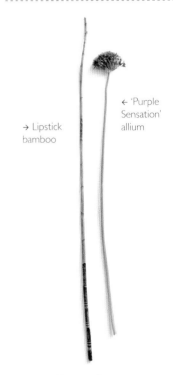

flowers

→ Lipstick bamboo

← 'Purple Sensation' allium

you will need

15 'Purple Sensation' alliums
1 long stem of lipstick or green bamboo

materials

Clear cellophane (optional)
Rectangular block of floral foam
Craft knife
1 cement trough 12x24cm (5x10in)
Florist's scissors
Secateurs

substitution

Gerberas or narcissi and snakegrass

Rose heart

An unashamedly romantic design, this heart-shaped spray rose arrangement is a fabulous gift for Mother's Day or Valentine's Day. Lay it flat on a coffee table, prop it up on a shelf or chair, or insert wire through the top of the foam before adding the flowers so you can hang it up.

how to arrange

1 Immerse the floral foam heart in a large bucket or sink full of water for about 3 minutes, until no more bubbles rise up and the foam is soaked through and feels heavy (don't oversoak it).

2 Separate the individual rose heads from their main stems and trim each short stem to 5cm (2in).

3 Starting at the top of the heart, insert each rose stem straight down into the flat foam. Add the roses in small sections, butting them right up against one another so the foam is completely concealed. Regularly stop to check your work. Use a mix of small, medium, and large blooms to give a random look on the front of the heart; you don't need to follow a pattern or regulate the size of the roses, although you can concentrate the smaller rose heads at the edges and sides if you want to.

4 Insert the remaining roses at the edges and around the sides of the foam. Insert these stems at a slight downwards angle so the flower heads point outwards to create curved corners and give the design a rounded shape.

 insider tips

• Water may leak from the base of the floral foam if you stand or hang it upright, so prop up the arrangement on a kitchen draining board once you have inserted the flowers so any excess water can drain away.

• The arrangement should last for six days if you mist the flowers every day.

flowers

← Pink spray roses

↑ Pale pink spray roses

Peach → spray roses

you will need

12 pink spray roses
12 pale pink spray roses
12 peach spray roses

materials

1 floral foam heart with a base, 25cm (10in) in diameter
Florist's scissors
Strong wire or thread if you want to hang the arrangement

Pink spray roses

Small-headed pink spray roses are an excellent choice for this compact arrangement, where the flowers butt right up against each other, because their stalks, once cut down, remain firm enough to insert into wet foam.

Miniature floral urn

With its deep, sumptuous colours and bountiful summer ingredients, this display is designed to be flamboyant, even though it is quite a tight, compact, small design. Choose cultivated clematis, which has long upright stems that are most suitable for flower arranging.

signature details

When seen sideways on, this front-facing arrangement is defined by its characteristic teardrop shape, with tall stems at the back of the vase to give height to the abundance of short-stemmed flowers, foliage, and fruit at the front and sides just above the urn. This is also a playful take on proportion: although it looks large and extravagant, the design is only 48cm (19in) tall, with the cherries, blackberries, and passion fruits tucked in among the rich purple and red blooms all helping to reveal the reality of the arrangement.

flowers and foliage

Old-fashioned spray rose →

Black ↓ flag iris

Cultivated purple clematis ↓

Sweet William ↓

↓ Blackberries

Cherries ↓

↑ Hebe

Passion fruit ↑

↑ Copper beech

you will need

1 copper beech stem
1 hebe stem
2 purple cultivated clematis
3 old-fashioned red spray roses
3 black flag iris
3 red sweet Williams
Dark fruits – 5 cherries, 5 blackberries, and 3 passion fruits

materials

1 miniature metal urn 21cm (8in) tall
Rectangle of floral foam
Clear cellophane
Craft knife
Florist's scissors
Wooden skewers and stub wires

for step by step, see overleaf

Miniature floral urn
step by step

Line the urn with clear cellophane to make it watertight. Cellophane is hard to see once trimmed and won't spoil the arrangement.

Trim the fruit sticks like flower stems with scissors or secateurs, cutting those at the front shorter than those at the back.

1 Cut the foam roughly to size, soak it in water (p161), and push it into the urn. Cut down the hebe and copper beech. Add 1 hebe stem at the centre back of the foam and 1 copper beech stem at either side, angling these stems downwards to create a skeleton framework.

2 Trim the cellophane. Add 6 more foliage stems to create a full, but airy, framework. Don't add all the foliage stems yet, as this is a small arrangement and you don't want to overfill the urn. Insert a wooden skewer into each passion fruit and press the cherries and blackberries onto stub wires. Insert some fruits into the centre of the design.

3 Arrange the rest of the fruits as a main cluster at the centre of the design, angling the skewers and stub wires downwards as you insert them so the fruits point upwards and outwards. Then add the stems of flag iris at the back and sides.

insider tips

• Rose stems are woody, so split them with florist's scissors before inserting them into the florist's foam.

• It's worth arranging this display on a towel or on a draining board: as you add more flowers, the foam will leach water out of the sides.

• A slim terracotta pot is a good alternative if you don't have an urn.

4 Add a mixture of rosebuds and semi-open and open roses, distributing them around the arrangement, but keeping the stems reasonably short so the blooms remain compact and close to the centre.

5 Add a few stems of sweet William. Its small flower petals make it quite a subtle flower for this arrangement, so its hint of pink and green tips provides more of a background detail than a feature.

6 Place tall stems of clematis at the back and insert the shortest stems at an upward angle at the front and sides so the flower heads hang down. Add a little more foliage to fill any obvious gaps.

The purple hue of the clematis is intense, so it makes sense to add it last and distribute it evenly throughout the arrangement.

Carnation balls

Everyday carnations become extraordinarily intricate designs of delicately textured petals when massed together. Make up several balls in harmonious colours.

flowers

← Dark-pink carnation

Lilac carnation
↓

you will need

120 dark-pink carnation stems
120 lilac carnation stems

materials

1 floral foam ball 20cm (8in)
    in diameter
1 floral foam ball 15cm (6in)
    in diameter
1 floral foam ball 11.5cm (5in)
    in diameter
Florist's scissors

how to arrange

1 Immerse the large foam ball in water for about 3 minutes (p161). Trim all the lilac carnation stems so they are 2.5cm (1in) in length.

2 Push the stems into the foam, butting them up to conceal the foam. Work in sections to cover the ball. Repeat with the other 2 balls.

 insider tips

• Leave the ball to drain for a while after you have arranged it, as water may continue to leach out. If you want to position this as a free-standing arrangement on a table, ensure the table is waterproof. Mist the flowers every day.

• Carnations can be gently teased open to make the flower heads look fuller, if you want to use fewer flowers.

Lilac carnations

Ordinary carnations come into their own when arranged en masse. Their robust petals can withstand being pushed close up against each other, and the slight variations in the lilac hues of the petals add extra depth.

Rose pyramid

flower

Dark-pink
spray rose →

Like a towering jelly on a plate, this almost edible design of pink roses is a perfect table centrepiece for a special meal or party, or make two to sit at either end of a mantelpiece.

how to arrange

you will need

20–25 stems dark-pink spray roses

materials
----

1 floral foam cone 32cm (13in) high
Florist's scissors

substitutions

White or pale-yellow spray roses

1 | Immerse the cone in water for about 3 minutes, until soaked through. Leave to drain. Trim the roses to single flower heads with 1cm (½in) stems and arrange into four piles according to size, from unopened buds to opened flowers.

2 | Insert a few unopened buds gently into the tip of the cone at an angle. Then, using the smallest buds first, press the rest of the flower heads straight into the foam (not at an angle) in concentric circles. Turn the cone in one direction as you work.

 insider tips

• As you insert more roses, water will seep out of the foam, so stand the cone on a waterproof surface, or on a plate, before you start arranging.

• Once filled with rosebud stems, the tip of the cone becomes very fragile. Try to avoid moving the finished arrangement too much. Mist the design daily.

Beach house flowers

Inspired by bleached driftwood and long sunny days, this cool, fresh all-round design is perfectly suited to a coffee table in a seaside house or as the centrepiece for a relaxed summer meal. These ingredients will withstand five to seven days in floral foam.

signature details

Contrasting textures, a limited palette of crisp, clean colours, and unusual ingredients make this an intriguing arrangement that looks good from every angle. Smooth-skinned apples on skewers and veined cabbage leaves have been mixed in among layers of white petals and lime-green flower heads and berries. Most of the ingredients are arranged at an angle to create a curved three-dimensional compact design that overhangs its container in a charming way.

flowers and foliage

White
↓ dahlia

↓ Ornamental
cabbage

Green
↓ hydrangea

Green
apple ↑

Green ↑
hypericum

← White
'Avalanche' rose

you will need

5 green hydrangeas
6 white 'Avalanche' roses
6 white dahlias
9 green hypericum stems
6 green apples
5 ornamental cabbages

materials

1 distressed white wooden basket
   about 15cm (6in) high and 30cm
   (12in) in diameter
Blocks of floral foam
Craft knife
Florist's scissors
Secateurs
Wooden skewers

for step by step, see overleaf

Beach house flowers
step by step

Check that the basket is watertight and line the inside with clear cellophane if necessary, trimming the ends after adding the wet foam.

The first 3 stems of hydrangea will help you testablish the height and width of the design, and how tall the rest of the stems should be.

1 Cut the foam approximately to size so it will fit in the basket, immerse it in water for 3 minutes or until no more bubbles rise up, and push it into place. Fill any gaps with more soaked foam. Trim the hydrangea stems to 10–12cm (4–5in). Insert 1 stem in the middle and 2 angled at the sides.

2 Check the length of the rose stems against the arranged hydrangeas before trimming and placing them in the foam. Insert them at an angle, distributing them evenly throughout the arrangement.

Trim the floral foam so it sits below the rim of the basket, rather than sitting proud, to ensure it will be completely concealed.

3 Add the dahlias, again checking the height of their stems before trimming them and placing them in the gaps. Turn the container as you work, so you build up an even distribution of blooms all the way around the design.

insider tips

• Cut and split the hydrangea and rose stems, stand them in a bucket of fresh water for an hour, then re-cut and split their stems just before arranging the flowers in the floral foam.

• Treat the ornamental cabbage and green hypericum as cut flowers: cut and condition them by giving them a long drink in the same bucket as the flowers.

To add a little variety and more detail, push some apples upside down onto the skewers and arrange others with their stalks showing.

4 Add the ornamental cabbages, interspersing them among the other flowers. This ingredient is fairly dominant, so don't overcrowd the design with it.

Trim any leaves from the thick stems of the ornamental cabbages so they are easier to insert into the foam.

5 Add the green hypericum in obvious gaps around the edges and through the centre. Add more hydrangeas and white flowers if you need to, trying to keep a balance of colour, shape, and texture throughout, but leaving enough space for the apples to fit in.

6 Push the end of a wooden skewer into the centre of an apple. Trim the other end of the skewer, as you would a flower stem, and insert it into the foam. Repeat with the rest of the apples.

White highlights

The cool white petals and almost lime-green centres of these symmetrical dahlias are set off to perfection against the crisp dark-green leaves of the ornamental cabbages that sit next to them.

Lisianthus cubes

flower

Pink lisianthus →

Rest some of these compact designs on their sides and sit others upright for a striking geometric display on a shelf or mantelpiece, or place them in a uniform line on a table.

how to arrange

you will need

----

20 stems of pink lisianthus

materials

----

4 black cube vases 12x12cm (5x5in)
Rectangles of floral foam
Craft knife
Florist's scissors

substitutions

Mini carnations
Rose buds
White vases with cream or
     purple lisianthus

1 Cut the foam roughly to fit each vase, immerse in water (p161), and push it into place. Cut off the individual flowers so their stems are 2.5cm (1in) long. Press 1 or 2 flower heads into one corner of the foam.

2 Add more flowers in straight lines, butting them up next to each other to conceal the foam. Their tips must create a flat, even surface, so adjust them if necessary. Repeat with the remaining flowers and vases.

 insider tips

• Once filled, rest those vases that you want to position on their sides on a draining board for a while first so that any excess water can drain away.

• Lisianthus petals bruise easily, so hold the flower heads at the base when you insert them into the foam.

Hydrangea table wreath

This compact seasonal table centrepiece of mixed flowers and foliage is a lush display of rounded shapes and bright colours. Once inserted into floral foam, the flowers should be misted daily to prevent them looking tired or drying out. They should last for five days.

flowers and foliage

↓ Blue hydrangea

Variegated pittosporum ↓

↑ Deep-pink spray rose

↑ Hebe   ← Pink rose

signature details

Harmonious colours of strong pink hues and blue predominate in this design, but they are carefully balanced by stems of green foliage, which are interspersed throughout the arrangement. The stems of both flowers and foliage are trimmed to the same length so they sit above the foam at the same height, creating a perfectly curved outline. If you don' t use a candle, insert more flowers and foliage into the inside of the wreath to conceal the foam.

you will need

3 hebe
3 variegated pittosporum stems
3 blue hydrangeas
6 pink roses
10–12 deep-pink spray roses

materials

1 floral foam ring with a base,
    24cm (10in) in diameter
Florist's scissors
1 large candle and candle holder
    (optional)

for step by step, see overleaf

Hydrangea table wreath
step by step

Cut the large hydrangeas into 3–4 smaller florets with short stems before arranging approximately 8 florets into the foam.

Angling the stems of the flowers and foliage upwards or downwards as you insert them helps to build up a smoothly rounded outline.

1 Immerse the foam ring in water for about 3 minutes (p161). Insert a few stems of each type of foliage into the foam in 3 equally spaced blocks. Work from the outside into the centre, inserting the stems around the outer edge at an upwards angle to cover the base.

2 Add the biggest flowers – the hydrangeas – first. Distribute them around the foam ring, inserting those near, or at, the edge at an upwards angle.

3 Add the large roses next, cutting their stems short and placing them in between the hydrangeas and foliage. Insert the stems at the corners of the foam at a downwards angle and those around the base at an upwards angle.

• Give the flowers and foliage a good drink in a bucket of water for an hour before inserting them into the floral foam.

• Trim the stems of the flowers and foliage down to 4–5cm (1½–2in) before arranging them, as this is intended to be quite a compact arrangement.

4 Cut the individual spray roses from their main stems, trim their short stems, and add them in small groups into the gaps, following the same technique. Check that you like the balance of blooms around the ring, and the distribution of colours, as you work.

5 Look for any obvious gaps in the design and fill them with some more short stems of foliage and spray roses.

6 Move the wreath into position on a dining room table or coffee table, and insert the candle holder and candle into the centre.

Use your judgement as to how many of each flower and foliage to use. They should be evenly interspersed and not overcrowded.

Planted designs

The designs in this chapter are a great way to make use of plants, which last longer than flowers. Some of these displays mix potted plants with flowers for a stylish effect and are known as "plantiques"; others show clever ways of presenting plants in a fun and attractive way.

Orchid tank

Perfect for a hall table, this orchid arrangement brings the outdoors inside with natural elements and textural details. Orchids like their roots to be cramped, so it's worth keeping them in their plastic pots and disguising the pots with more interesting materials.

signature details

Orchids bring a touch of exotic delicacy with their brightly coloured, fleshy petals, but their semi-translucent pots are not appealing to look at. This design is built up around the pot with a base of carpet moss, a screen of terracotta and birch bark, and a spray of birch twigs that create three-dimensional shape and form and give substance to the long thin-stemmed orchids. The small detail of raffia tied around plant stems is an attractive touch that repeats throughout the arrangement.

plants and foliage

Birch twig ↓

Phalaenopsis orchid ↓

↑ Carpet moss

you will need

1 phalaenopsis orchid
1 bunch (approximately 10) birch twigs
Carpet moss
2 medium-sized old broken terracotta pots
2 miniature terracotta pots
1 piece of birch bark

materials

1 large square straight-sided vase, approximately 30cm (12in) tall
Hammer
Kitchen towel or leaf shine
Raffia

for step by step, see overleaf

Orchid tank
step by step

To break up a pot, ensure your eyes are
protected and use a hammer to carefully
knock away sections of the sides and rim.

Trim the birch bark, if necessary, so that it fits
snugly inside the pot, but so that enough of
its textural surface detail is still visible.

1 Sit the orchid pot under
running water for 5 minutes
and leave to drain. Place a layer of
carpet moss in the base of the
vase and add the pieces of pot in
a stack to build a structural base
for the orchid pot to sit on.

2 Set aside 4 of the birch twigs and tie
the rest in a bunch with raffia. Hold
the bunch against the vase, trim it so the
twigs will branch out above the rim, and
place it in the front corner of the vase.

3 Curl the piece of birch bark inside
the broken terracotta pot behind
the spray of twigs so it covers the gap
in the pot and will provide an effective
screen for the plastic orchid pot.

Wind the raffia several times around the
bunch of twigs to make a thick binding, then
secure it in a knot and trim off the ends.

• If you give the orchid a drink under running water for 5 minutes before potting it up in the display, you should just need to refresh the plant with ½ teacup of water once a week until the flowers drop off.

• When the orchid has stopped flowering, cut it off just above a node. It will grow again from this point, so cut it as low as you want the regrowth to start. In six to nine months, new stems will grow and flowers should appear.

4 If the orchid leaves need it, give them a wipe with a piece of damp kitchen towel or use leaf shine. Place the orchid pot inside the broken pot behind the birch bark.

5 Trim the 4 remaining birch twigs slightly and insert them into the back of the orchid pot so they stand upright and fan out behind the flowers. Remove the orchid flower stakes.

6 Using raffia, tie 1 orchid stem to a birch twig behind it. Repeat with the other orchid stem. Rest the mini terracotta pots on top of the orchid pot and add moss in front.

Once attached to a birch twig with a short length of raffia, the orchid stems will lean out to each side in a graceful curve.

Preserved plants

plants

Miniature
phalaenopsis
orchid →

Fasciata
'Haworthia' →

Plants rather than flowers are used for this design as they last longer – from one month to several months – and so are almost "preserved" inside their vases and storage jars.

how to arrange

you will need

3 miniature phalaenopsis orchids
2 fasciata 'Haworthia'
1 clear glass column vase 20cm (8in) tall
   15cm (6in) wide
1 clear glass column vase 25cm (10in) tall
   12cm (5in) wide
1 clear glass column vase 30cm (12in) tall
   10cm (4in) wide
2 large glass preserving jars 17–18cm
   (7in) tall and 7–12cm (3–5in) wide
Multi-purpose compost

Substitution

Spring bulbs such as muscari or narcissi

1 Fill the vase or jar with soil to the same depth as the orchid pot – about 8cm (3in). Make a hole in the centre of the soil. Remove the orchid from its pot and tease out its roots to loosen them a little.

2 Remove the garden stick and clip from the orchid and plant it in the hole. Cover any gaps around the edge of the planted orchid with soil, using your hand, or the stick if the vase is narrow. Repeat with the other plants.

 insider tips

• If your jars or vases are quite narrow in diameter, use a garden stick to make the well in the centre and flick the soil in place around the plant.

• Give the orchids a drink under running water for five minutes before you plant them, and give all the plants a good misting once a week.

Bulbs in a cheese pot

The thin round wooden cheese pots that contain soft cheeses like Camembert can be turned into delightful rustic containers for potted bulbs. This delicate, pared-back design suits a bedside table or bathroom, where you can easily catch the fragrant scent of lily of the valley.

how to arrange

1 Line the cheese pot with cellophane to make it water resistant.

2 Carefully turn out the potted lily of the valley and cut across the base of the roots in a straight line with scissors, so the bulb roots in soil are half the depth they were in the pot

3 Gently transfer the bulbs in their soil to the lined cheese pot and press them firmly into place. Mist the soil to dampen it sufficiently.

4 Using scissors, trim the edges of the cellophane so it can't be seen. Cover the top of the pot with carpet moss to hide all evidence of the dark soil, and give the moss a good misting again.

insider tip

• The arrangement should last for at least two weeks if you mist the moss and flowers every couple of days, especially in warm weather, to keep the soil moist and the leaves and flowers looking fresh.

flower and foliage

Lily of
the valley →

Carpet moss →

you will need

1 pot of lily of the valley
Carpet moss

materials

1 round wooden cheese pot
Clear cellophane
Florist's scissors

substitution

Flowering muscari bulbs

Succulent garden

Fleshy succulents make excellent house plants. Why not encourage children to design and plant their own miniature succulent garden in an old cake tin; there is a wide selection of interesting small succulents to choose from, and they don't need much water or care.

signature details

This long-lasting display, with its echoes of bonsai, is a take on a Japanese Zen garden, where simple natural elements arranged in a pattern give a sense of calm and order. The stylized landscape is created with a limited selection of ingredients: planted succulents overlap the edges of the cake tin and build in height from the front of the tin to a magnolia "tree" at the rear, and perspective is created by a winding path that narrows as it disappears into the back of the design. The detail of a dogwood picket fence gives a delightful finishing touch to this miniature design.

plants and foliage

↑ Crassula 'Ovata'

← Dogwood stem

↑ Kalanchoe

Magnolia twig with buds ↓

↑ Echeveria

↑ Crassula

you will need

1 crassula 'Ovata'
1 kalanchoe
1 echeveria
1 crassula
1 magnolia twig with buds
2 dogwood stems

materials

1 old cake tin with a fixed base
Multi-purpose compost
White gravel
Secateurs

for step by step, see overleaf

Succulent garden
step by step

Don't overfill the tin with soil at this stage; you will be planting 4 succulents and adding more soil later on.

Keep a curved area through the centre of the tin plant free for a path, although it's up to you exactly where you want the path to be.

I Fill the tin nearly to the rim with soil. Make a hole in the soil at the edge of the tin and plant a short succulent, such as a crassula, in the hole so its leaves overlap the edge of the tin. Gently firm the soil around the plant with your fingertips.

2 Choose a slightly taller succulent, such as a crassula 'Ovata', to sit behind the short succulent. Make a second hole in the soil at the edge of the tin for the plant and firm the soil around it.

3 Plant another short succulent, such as an echeveria, on the other side of the tin, making sure its leaves overlap the edge of the tin. Plant the slightly taller kalanchoe just behind it.

If you don't want to get too much soil on your hands, wear thin gardening gloves to plant each of the succulents.

insider tips

• Choose an old cake tin with a fixed base so that no soil can escape.

• The joy of planting succulents is that they survive without too much watering, although you can try other plants if you can care for them. As the cake tin has no drainage holes, it's best not to use plants that need lots of water.

• Drizzle a few drops of water over each plant and mist their leaves at least once a week. If they fade or die, you can easily replace them with another succulent.

4 Top up the tin with more soil to just below the rim. Sketch the outline of a path through the planted succulents with a few pieces of the white gravel.

Try to create a gently winding path that becomes wider as it nears the front of the container to give an illusion of perspective.

5 When you are happy with the shape of the path, fill it in with more gravel. Cut the dogwood into 6 lengths, each 10cm (4in) long. Insert 5 stems into the soil in a line by the path, and weave the last piece horizontally in between the upright stems to create a picket fence.

6 Add the stem of magnolia buds at the back of the arrangement to give the appearance of a small tree. Mist the succulents well with a hand mister.

Use the middle sections of the long dogwood stems (the tips are too thin and the bases too thick) and strip off any side shoots.

Succulents and roses

By washing their roots free of soil, succulents can be used in a florist's foam arrangement like cut flowers. These rosette plants blend beautifully with coral-coloured roses in a compact display that is determined by the shape and curves of the vase. It should last for four to six days.

how to arrange

1 Half-fill the vase with scrunched cellophane or a bin liner. Hold the block of foam against the vase and cut it roughly to size so it will sit at least 8cm (3in) above the rim to create some height. Immerse the foam in water (p161) and then push it into place in the vase. If there are any gaps, add more soaked pieces of foam.

2 Tip the succulents out of their pots, shake off the excess soil, and wash their roots under running water. Wind a length of wire around each short root base so they are easier to insert into the foam. Distribute the plants around the design.

3 Trim the stems of the roses to 5cm (2in) and add them in clusters so they match the size of the largest succulent heads.

4 Cut the stems of the sedum to 5cm (2in) and tuck them into the foam around the succulents and roses.

5 Place the bridal blush and echeveria flowers into the gaps in the foam. Insert any stems near the rim of the vase at an upwards angle to conceal the foam.

insider tips

• Mist the leaves and flowers every day to prolong their life.

• The succulents will last longer than the cut flowers, so they can be reused in another arrangement.

flowers

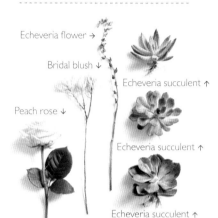

Echeveria flower →
Bridal blush ↓
Echeveria succulent ↑
Peach rose ↓
Echeveria succulent ↑
Echeveria succulent ↑
← Pink rose   ← Sedum

you will need

10 sedum stems
6 peach roses
6 pink roses
5 bridal blush
7 echeveria flowers
7 mixed echeveria succulents

materials

1 curved opaque textured
   vase 24x25cm (9½x10in)
Cellophane or bin liner
1 floral foam block
Craft knife
Florist's scissors
Stub wire

Textural contrasts

Highly textural designs reveal a wealth of detail. Here, unusual small flowers – bright-green sedum, spire-shaped echeveria, and bridal blush, with their spiky star-shaped petals – intermingle with smooth layers of rose petals.

Plantique with tulips

We use the term "plantique" for our long-lasting base designs of potted plants that incorporate freshly cut flowers, which are replaced every few days. This verdant display is an easy way to create a semi-permanent arrangement in the heart of your home.

signature details

A design like this doesn't require expert skills or techniques, just a good eye for balancing shapes, textures, and sizes. The plants and flowers are positioned to create a balance of shapes and look as natural as possible together, and are given cohesion with a blanket of carpet moss. This plantique lasts indefinitely if you refresh the potted calla lily and greenery under running water weekly, re-cut the flower stems to prolong their life, and change the flowers when they are past their best. In this way, you can move through the seasons and even vary the colour scheme.

flowers

White calla lilies ↓

Yellow tulips ↓

Trailing ivy ↓

← Mind-your-own-business

↑ Muehlenbeckia   ↑ Carpet moss

you will need

1 pot white calla lilies
20 yellow tulips
1 small pot trailing ivy
3 small pots mind-your-own-business
1 small pot muehlenbeckia
Carpet moss

materials

Craft knife
Florist's scissors
Bin liners
Seagrass cord
1 large wooden box

for step by step, see overleaf

Plantique with tulips
step by step

Arrange scrunched-up bin liners so they provide an elevated base for the pots and vase and make the box watertight.

1 Line the box with bin liners. Sit the calla lily at the back-left corner just below the edge of the box, so only the stems and flowers rise up above the rim.

2 Slit the necks of the tulips with a craft knife and trim the bases of the stems to the same length with scissors. Arrange them loosely in a flared vase. Place the vase at the front-right corner of the box.

3 Place the small pot of trailing ivy at the front left of the box so it sits in front of the potted calla lilies and its stems cascade over the edge of the box and down the front.

Slit the neck of each tulip with a craft knife before arranging, to stop the tulips growing and help prevent their heads from drooping.

Scrunch up more bin liners, or even plastic bags, and place them under the pot to achieve the correct level for it to sit.

insider tips

• Stand the pot of calla lilies in water for 30–60 minutes to give it a good soak before you start work on the design.

• Use any container – an orange box, wicker basket, or a large wide-necked bowl, for instance – to create either an all-round or front-facing arrangement, depending on where you want to position it in a room.

• Refresh the green colour of the carpet moss by placing it in a sink, pouring over a kettle of boiling water, and leaving it to drain.

Press the carpet moss into the corners of the box and over the top of the arrangement so the different elements blend together.

4 Build up the gaps around the plant pots and vase with more bin liners if necessary. Place the small pots of mind your own business at the front and the muehlenbeckia near the back.

5 Use plenty of carpet moss to cover the exposed workings of the design – for example, any gaps where the bin liners show, and over the tops of the pots.

6 If the box will benefit from it, wind a length of seagrass cord around the outside a couple of times and tie the cord in a simple knot.

Tuck the pots of mind-your-own-business in the gap between the calla lilies and tulips to fill the empty space.

Mist the flowers and foliage with a spray mist every day to keep the leaves and blooms looking fresh, especially in warm weather.

Large-scale designs

Changing the scale of an arrangement brings a new level of drama to your environment. These impressive designs are all very straightforward: they use the same approaches, techniques, and types of container explored in other chapters, but on a grand scale, to give that "wow" factor.

Delphinium layered vase

Everything about this front-facing vase arrangement is on a grand scale. The layered rather than distributed flowers and foliage are all large blooms and leaves, and the colour palette is intentionally daring and eye-catching. This display will last for four to six days.

Unusually for a front-facing vase arrangement, the shape of this design is quite top-heavy when seen from the side, with a mass of lilac delphiniums fanning out at the top. A strong palette of both complementary and harmonious colours creates a striking effect of concentrated hues that emphasize the layers of different flowers. Concealing all the stems in the vase with a monstera leaf is a neat detail that makes a feature of the vase and adds more greenery to the arrangement.

flowers and foliage

Pink lily ↓   Lilac delphinium ↓

Lime-green hydrangea ↓

Copper beech ↓

↑ Monstera leaf

you will need

17 lilac delphinium
5 pink lilies
12 lime-green hydrangeas
2 copper beech leaf stems
4 monstera leaves

materials

1 clear glass vase, either an urn or
   column vase, 45cm (18in) tall
Florist's scissors
Sterilizing tablet

for step by step, see overleaf →

Delphinium layered vase
step by step

Carefully slide the monstera leaf into the vase, tip first, until the tip reaches the bottom. Then spread out the leaf inside the vase.

Don't worry about any lily buds that rise up above the layer of lilies – they should enhance rather than detract from the design.

1 Place 1 monstera leaf vertically inside the front of the vase, to screen as many of the flower stems as possible. Cut off the leaf stem once the monstera is arranged in place.

2 Half-fill the vase with water and add a sterilizing tablet. Arrange 3 more monstera leaves – 1 at the front and 1 at either side – so their stems cross and the leaves rest on the rim of the vase. These leaves provide a support frame for the rest of the design.

3 Carefully remove the stamens from the lilies (p27). Trim their long stems to the same height and place them in the vase so the flowers sit just above the monstera leaves.

Cut off or pinch out the stamens from the lilies (wear rubber gloves) to prevent the yellow pollen from staining petals and clothes.

insider tips

• Wipe the monstera leaves with leaf shine or a damp cloth for added impact.

• When adding the flowers, ensure their stems don't poke through the monstera leaf lining the inside the vase.

> Once the lily buds start to open, they will stand out against the delphiniums and become an extra layer in the arrangement.

> If any layers look slightly unbalanced once you have finished, add the odd flower or foliage stem to even out the symmetrical design.

4 Hold the stems of the hydrangeas up against the side of the vase to gauge how long to trim them. Arrange the hydrangeas in a layer so they form a line of lime green running above the pink lily petals. The hydrangeas should literally "sit" on top of the lily heads.

5 Hold the delphiniums against the vase to see where to trim them; the flowers should rise up from the heads of the hydrangeas. The stems should be as upright as possible, so add more flower stems if necessary. These stems will be supported further by the copper beech.

6 Cut the long copper beech stems to make several shorter stems and insert them among the delphiniums to both support them and add a foil of darker foliage. The deep tones of these leaves are matched by the dark stamens at the centres of the delphinium flowers.

Gypsophila vases

flower and foliage

Black tie leaf →

↑ White gypsophila

Clouds of tiny gypsophila can be turned into sculptural, almost architectural designs if they are used en masse and given minimalist treatment. This is a real statement piece.

how to arrange

you will need

3 black tie leaves
2 very large bunches of white gypsophila
    (about 50 stems in total)

materials

1 clear glass column vase 50×14cm
    (20×5½in)
2 very large white ceramic vases
Clear cellophane
Florist's scissors

1 Add loosely scrunched cellophane to the lower half of the vase, and half-fill with water. Cut the end off each black tie leaf and line the vase with the upright leaves, overlapping them so they hide the cellophane. Add more cellophane so it fills most of the vase. Add more water.

2 Cut the tips off leaves that sit above the rim of the vase. Trim a bunch of gypsophila stems, so that once placed on top of the cellophane they start branching out naturally above the rim of the vase. Repeat with the rest of the gypsophila and the other two vases.

 insider tip

• Gypsophila stems can become easily tangled. Carefully separate the stems and "fluff" them out, so they are at their fullest when you arrange them. Keep any cut-offs to make up smaller displays for a side table or bathroom shelf.

White gypsophila

Gypsophila is easy to identify, as its long main stems carry
a large number of very slender offshoot stems that are
covered in a huge abundance of tiny flowers. Each
star-like flower has a tiny yellow-green centre.

Stacked dogwood stems

foliage

← Green dogwood

Red dogwood →

This minimalist, highly sculptural stacked design of swirling dogwood looks stunning placed on the floor of a living room or dining room. The stems last for two weeks.

how to arrange

I Cut off the thick end of each stem, leaving 80cm (32in) to work with, and trim off all side shoots. Divide the green dogwood in half so there are 10 green stems each for 2 vases. The third vase will contain the red stems.

2 Press the end of a stem into the base of the vase. Bend and twist it into a spiral pattern so it rises up and down around the edge of the vase. Turn the vase slightly after adding each stem to create a framework effect. Repeat with the rest of the dogwood.

you will need

Approximately 10 red dogwood stems
Approximately 20 green dogwood stems

materials

Florist's scissors or secateurs
3 large clear glass fish bowl vases

substitution

Birch twigs or pussy willow
Alternatively, pour water into each vase, add a sterilizing tablet, and leave the stems to sprout lime-green leaves. Refresh the water every week.

 insider tips

• Watch out for your face and eyes as you twist the sharp ends of the dogwood stems into place.

• Keep the thicker base of each stem at or near the base of the vase.

• Use very fresh dogwood, as it will bend easily.

Floating orchids with a hat

The dramatic design and deep colour scheme of this arrangement suits a party table centre or a hall console table, where its stunning three-dimensional display can be seen from every angle. Alternatively, arrange in pairs on the floor. The flower heads should last for one week.

signature details

A voluminous hat of closely packed hydrangea flowers set in florist's foam tops this large-scale arrangement of orchid flowers, which are submerged in water and tethered using bright-pink wire, so that plenty of space exists around each flower head. The arrangement should look attractive from every side, so the wire helps to keep each orchid in place, facing out through the walls of the clear glass vase.

flowers

← Purple hydrangea

Blue-purple 'Vanda' orchid heads →

you will need

10–12 purple hydrangeas
12–15 blue-purple 'Vanda' orchid heads

materials

1 floral foam ball 25cm (10in)
   in diameter
Pink reel wire
Florist's scissors
1 flared glass vase 70cm (28in) tall
Sterilizing tablet

substitution

'Vanda' orchids are available in a wide
   variety of colours; match the colour of
   the hydrangea to the orchid

 *for step by step, see overleaf*

Floating orchids with a hat
step by step

The foam ball will leach out water for a while once soaked, so arrange the hydrangeas first to prevent green sediment filling the vase.

Cut the orchid flower from its main stem and place the wire hook against the side of the flower stalk, not around it.

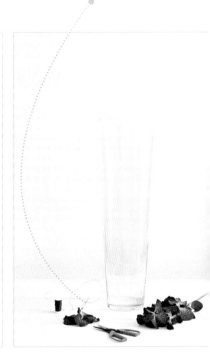

I Immerse the foam ball in water (p161). Cut each hydrangea into 4–5 small florets and trim each stem to 5cm (2in). Insert a few stems into the top of the foam, 5–6cm (2–2½in) apart.

2 Cover the top and sides of the foam ball with the hydrangeas, setting aside a few of the florets for later and leaving the base of the ball free of flowers. Set the foam ball aside to drain.

3 To wire an orchid, cut a length of wire 20cm (8in) long. Make a small hook at one end and place it against the side of 1 orchid flower stalk. Gently wind the long end of the wire a few times around the stalk and hook. Repeat with the rest of the orchid flowers and wire.

Butt the florets of hydrangea petals up against each other so the foam ball beneath is completely concealed.

insider tips

• Handle the orchids with care so you don't bruise the petals.

• Hydrate the hydrangea by misting it and drizzling a little water over the foam ball (hydrangea petals don't mind being sprinkled with water).

• The vase will probably be too large to be filled with water in a sink, so use a jug or empty water bottle to gradually add more water as you build the design.

Add a little more scrunched wire to the top of the vase if you need to press down any orchids that are floating on top.

4 Add water to a height of 15cm (6in), and a sterilizing tablet. Loosely scrunch a length of wire and drop it into the vase. Place a wired orchid on top of the wire frame.

5 Add more water and layer more wire and orchids in the half-filled vase. Keep adding water as you fill the vase to the top with orchids and wire.

6 Place the hydrangea ball on top of the vase. Insert the reserved hydrangea stems at an upward angle into the base of the foam ball to hide the rim of the vase.

Position the orchid near the edge of the vase, facing out. The scrunched wire creates a framework for it to rest on, so it doesn't sink.

Use a stick or garden cane to nudge any flowers into position, so their petals are fully open and they are spaced evenly in the water.

Purple hydrangeas

When seen close up, the petals of these purple
hydrangeas reveal almost geometric individual flowers,
with delicate deep-purple veins that run from the tip of
each petal down to a tiny blue–purple centre.

Giant gladioli

Eighty stems of lilac gladioli create this spectacular, but incredibly easy, display. To fill a container this size would take many more gladioli, so the space inside is restricted by a raised bucket, which creates the right shape for the long stems to flare out. If you keep topping up the water regularly, the flowers will last for five to seven days.

how to arrange

1 Place 1 bucket upside down inside the container and wedge it into place with bin liners or large pieces of polystyrene.

2 Position the second bucket on top of the upturned bucket and add some more padding around it so it won't topple over. Half-fill the upright bucket with water.

3 Trim all the gladioli stems to the same length, leaving as much of the stem intact as possible, so you keep a dramatic sense of height. Add the stems to the bucket, about 20 stems at a time, tweaking them into place to create a gently flared shape. Top up the water if needed.

insider tips

• Strip the lower leaves from the base of each flower stem; fewer leaves will mean more of the water goes to the flowers themselves.

• As there is a large quantity of flowers in this design, they will drink up water quickly. Check the water level regularly, and top it up as needed.

flower

Lilac gladioli →

you will need

80 long-stemmed lilac gladioli

materials

1 opaque flared container, at least 55cm (22in) tall
2 large buckets that will fit inside the container
Bin liners or other lightweight padding
Florist's scissors or secateurs

Hydrangea and birch vase

This organic vase arrangement, which is designed to look like a living tree, can be as large as you like if you have a strong column vase that is big enough. If you refresh the water and replace the hydrangeas around the rim of the vase every week, the display should last for two weeks.

how to arrange

1 Place the covered vase in position on the floor of a living room, dining room, or hallway and half-fill it with water.

2 Stand 1 birch pole on the floor next to the vase, gauge how tall it should be, and saw off any excess. Repeat with the other 2 birch poles. The 3 birch poles should be differing heights, with the tallest pole about 3 times the height of the vase and the shortest pole just less than twice its height. Place the poles in the vase.

3 Distribute the birch twigs evenly between and around the poles, which provide the structure of the arrangement.

4 Re-cut and split the birch leaf and hydrangea stems. Add the birch leaf stems first, arranging them in the vase so their leaves branch out at either side.

5 Tuck the long hydrangea stems inside the vase and rest the flower heads on the rim to conceal the top of the vase. Fill to the brim with water.

insider tips

• Cut and split the hydrangea and birch leaf stems (pp24–25) and give them a long drink in deep water for an hour before re-cutting and splitting the stems and arranging them in the vase.

• Mist the hydrangea flowers every day to prolong their life. If the flower heads suddenly start to wilt, revive them by placing them upside down in a bucket of cold water for 30 minutes (p27).

flowers and foliage

← Birch leaves

Birch twig →

↑ Birch pole   ↑ 'Emerald Jewel' hydrangea

you will need

1 birch pole approximately 240cm (8ft)
  long, cut into 3 varying lengths
5 stems birch leaf
3 bunches birch twigs
5 'Emerald Jewel' hydrangeas

materials

1 birch bark-covered tall column vase
  at least 50cm (20in) tall
Hand saw
Florist's scissors

Lilac stack

A design such as this is all about harmonious colour and interesting textures. Tones of lilac, purple, and pink petals cover a large curved block of floral foam, which matches the shape of the container it stands on, to create a high stack of mixed blooms. It will last for five days.

signature details

There is no focal flower and no fixed method – such as layering or arranging in concentric circles – for this all-round compact display. Instead, the flowers are placed in a random, aesthetically pleasing way, with the flowers distributed around the foam so that no two varieties sit next to each other. All the stems are cut very short so the flower heads sit flush against the side of the foam column to create a uniform surface with a wonderful variety of textural detail.

flowers

Pink germini →

Purple hydrangea ↓

↑ Purple trachelium

Lilac statice →

Lilac 'Anastasia' ↑ chrysanthemum

you will need

20 purple trachelium
6 purple hydrangeas
25 pink germini (mini gerbera)
12 lilac 'Anastasia' chrysanthemums
25 lilac statice

materials

1 column of floral foam 40cm (16in) tall and 25cm (10in) wide
Florist's scissors
1 large curved vase 40cm (16in) tall and 25cm (10in) wide

for step by step, see overleaf

Lilac stack
step by step

Arrange the group of small hydrangea florets together so the stems are 1cm (½in) apart, and space the groups around the foam.

Don't feel compelled to use all the flowers of each variety at once; it's best to set aside a couple of each type of flower to fill gaps later.

1 Immerse each end of the foam in water (p161). Cut the hydrangeas into small florets with stems of 2cm (¾in). Press 2–3 stems at a time into the foam.

2 Trim the chrysanthemum stems to 3cm (1¼in) and insert these large individual flower heads into the sides and top of the foam.

3 Cut down the gerbera stems to 3cm (1¼in). These flowers have a more saturated colour than the hydrangeas and chrysanthemums, so make sure they are well distributed around the foam and not clumped too close together.

There are 5 or so large florets on a hydrangea flower; cut each large floret into 3–4 small florets that sit more neatly against the foam.

• A piece of soaked floral foam this size is very heavy and is hard to move around. If possible, make up the arrangement in situ. If you want to use this design as a table arrangement without the vase, it's best to place the foam on a dish, as it will leach out water. Have a towel or kitchen towel to hand if the dish is shallow, as water may overflow onto the table.

• Set aside a few of each variety of flower; as this is a large arrangement, you will need to build up the arrangement steadily and all round before filling in the gaps with a variety of each flower.

4 Trachelium is quite delicate and translucent, so, to make it appear a little more dense, add the flower heads in pairs to give the impression of 1 large flower head.

5 Cut down the branched stems of statice to short individual stems and insert them into the foam in bunches of 3 stems at a time.

6 Fill in the gaps with any reserved flowers. As the flowers vary in size, use the statice as a filler for the smallest spaces. Mist the flowers with a hand mister.

> Distribute the individual or grouped flower heads randomly for an asymmetrical display, but ensure that no two varieties sit together.

> Try to cover the base of the dish by angling the flower stems slightly upwards as you insert them around the bottom of the foam.

Eremurus border

Replicating the structure of a flower border, this out-sized arrangement features a row of tall eremurus along the back of a trough with potted lime-green hydrangeas spilling over the front. This design looks best on the floor against a wall, as if it were a real flower border growing indoors.

how to arrange

1 Line the inside of the trough with cellophane. Immerse each block of foam in water for about 3 minutes, until no more bubbles rise up (don't over-soak them), then position them in a line along the back of the trough. If there are any gaps at the back of the trough, fill them with more pieces of soaked foam.

2 Scrunch up more cellophane and wedge it into the long gap in front of the blocks. This will help to press the blocks against the back of the trough so that when the eremurus are inserted into the foam the blocks won't tip forwards. The cellophane also raises the height of the base for the hydrangea pots to sit on.

4 Place the pots of hydrangea in a line on top of the scrunched cellophane, so the pots themselves are hidden inside the trough and the green petals form an even line along the front of the trough.

5 Insert the eremurus along the length of the foam at the back of the trough in a zigzag line and at slightly different heights. Cover the workings of the design on the top and at the corners of the trough with a layer of carpet moss.

insider tips

• Cut and split the eremurus stems and stand them in a bucket of cool water for at least one hour before placing them in the floral foam.

• Stand the hydrangea pots in a sink half-filled with water for at least 20 minutes before arranging them. If you drizzle water over the foam and the pots every other day, and mist the flowers daily, the arrangement should last for one week.

flowers

Eremurus →

Lime-green
hydrangea pot ↓

Carpet moss ↑

you will need

6 lime-green hydrangea pots
16 eremurus
Carpet moss

materials

Clear cellophane
Florist's scissors
4 large oblong floral foam blocks
1 cement trough 20cm (8in) tall,
   20cm (8in) deep, and 87cm (35in) long

Green hydrangeas

The flower heads of this variety of hydrangea are unusual in that they have double petals, which gives them a particularly dense, ruffled look. Tones of pale green through to almost purple give the petals added interest.

Indoor flower garden

A larger version of a standard plantique (pp206–09), this combination of cut flowers and plants is a summery mix of blooms that, together, form a small indoor garden. The lavenders, godetia, miniature roses, and dahlias in pastel shades will look good for one week or more.

signature details

Keeping this arrangement fresh and natural are an attractive mix of cut and potted flowers in pastel colours that are offset by the bright green hues of carpet moss and leaves. Although it can be made up as an all-round arrangement, this display is slightly graduated to show off all the blooms when viewed from the front and sides. Ideal for a big fireplace, the display will last for up to a month if you change the cut flowers once they are past their best – or break it up after a week or two and plant the potted flowers outside in a garden border or window box.

for step by step, see overleaf

flowers

Pink godetia →

French lavender ↓

Pale yellow dahlia ↓

Miniature pink rose ↑

you will need

20 pale yellow dahlias
20 pink godetias
5 potted miniature pink roses
7 potted French lavender
Carpet moss

materials

1 large metal bath
3 column and/or flared vases, all just shorter than the height of the metal bath
Bin liners or cellophane

Indoor flower garden
step by step

Stand 2 vases in a line at the back of the metal bath and 1 vase at the front to create a triangular arrangement of containers.

Keep the godetia to hand as you trim the dahlias to check that their stems are long enough to match those of the cut dahlias.

1 Put the bath in position, as it will be heavy once finished. Half-fill the vases with water and arrange them in the centre of the bath. Scrunch up the cellophane or bin liners and press in around the vases to hold them in place and fill the base of the bath.

2 Arrange the cut flowers first. Strip the lower leaves from the dahlia stems and remove any withered lower petals. Fill 2 of the vases with dahlias, trimming the stems of those in the front vase short enough for the flowers to sit just above the rim of the bath. The dahlias in the vase behind should sit just above the flowers in front of them.

3 Arrange the godetia in a bouquet using a spiral stem technique (pp36–37). Trim their stems and place the bunch in the third vase, so the godetia stand midway in height between the two levels of dahlias.

insider tip

• Stand the potted plants in a sink half-filled with water for 10 minutes before using them. If you mist the flowers every day, pour a little water into the plants every week and replace the cut flowers, the design should last for one month.

Add more cellophane if you need to raise the height of the potted plants further, especially at the back, so all the flowers can be seen.

Distribute the pots of French lavender evenly around the design, so they balance out the blocks of pink and yellow flowers.

4 Arrange the potted miniature roses in blocks by eye: add 2 pots at the front-right of the bath and one at the front-left. Rest the plants on the scrunched cellophane so their pots are hidden just below the rim of the container.

5 Fill the gaps in between the potted roses and cut flowers with pots of lavender. The mauve and lilac hues of the lavender flowers and their bright green leaves and stems will help to draw all the pastel hues together.

6 Cover the surface of the arrangement with carpet moss, hiding all the cellophane and the pot rims and bringing another green hue into the design.

Peony madness

With their fluttering, multi-layered petals and large, fully blown shape, peonies are one of the best varieties for a large-scale arrangement using just one type of flower. Choose both single- and double-headed varieties in pale and bright pinks and deep reds for a fabulous impact.

how to arrange

1 Choose which column vases you want to line with green tie leaves, and which to line with the shorter hosta leaves. Insert the leaves carefully, curling them inside the vases and pressing them against the sides of the glass so no gaps are visible. Fill all the vases with water and add ½ sterilizing tablet to each clear glass vase.

2 Each small column vase will need 4–5 flowers, while the large vases and fishbowl will require 8–9 peonies. Restrict yourself to just one peony colour per vase. Keep the stems of the peonies for the leaf-covered vases as long as possible and arrange them loosely to create an attractive domed shape.

3 The peonies for the shorter vases need to be arranged using a spiral stem technique (pp36–37) and tied, as the flower heads are large and heavy and may tip out of the vase otherwise. Use a length of pink wire to tie each bunch, then trim the stems at an angle and place in a vase. Repeat with the remaining peonies.

4 Position the vases in a random, but pleasing, arrangement across a large table, placing the taller vases at the back. If you trim the stems and change the water after three days, the flowers should last for one week.

insider tip

• Peony petals are very fragile, so be careful when arranging the flowers right next to each other, especially if they are fully open.

flowers and foliage

→ Pale-pink peony

↓ Coral peony

← Pink peony

↑ Green tie leaf

Hosta leaf →

← Red peony

you will need

7 pale-pink 'Sandra Bernhardt' peonies
9 'Pink charm' peonies
4 coral peonies
8 'Red charm' peonies
5 green tie leaves
5 large variegated hosta leaves
3 small variegated hosta leaves

materials

Florist's scissors
Pink wire
7 clear glass column vases 18–50cm
   (7–20in) tall
1 clear glass fish bowl vase
Sterilizing tablets

Red peonies

The rich red colour of these extravagant peonies is shown off to perfection when they are arranged together. The centre of each peony is remarkable once opened fully, as it reveals a mass of tiny, textured petals.

Hydrangea garland

This arrangement, running the full length of a table, is a real show-stopper for a celebration or party. Add the flowers and foliage bit by bit, until the garland matches the length of your table, and make it fairly last-minute, as it will only look its best for 24 hours.

Large globes of deep-pink petals provide a fabulous visual contrast to clusters of tiny iridescent green flowers in this vivid complementary colour design. The flowers are layered on top of dark-green deeply veined leaves to create a sumptuous table display, and the hydrangea heads are angled out at either side to accentuate the three-dimensional shape of this design.

for step by step, see overleaf

flowers and foliage

← Aralia leaf

Hydrangea leaf ↓

Pink → hydrangea

Alchemilla mollis →

you will need

Depending on the length of your table, you will need at least:
2 aralia leaves
5 stems of hydrangea foliage
3 pink hydrangeas
20 alchemilla mollis

materials

Long length of rope or sash cording
Florist's scissors
Garden string

substitution

White or red roses arranged in groups of three for a Christmas display

Hydrangea garland
step by step

Ensure the flowers and foliage have a really good drink beforehand, as this is a temporary design and none of the stems will be in water.

Pull the string tight before wrapping it around another stem, otherwise the garland will become too loose and floppy to handle.

1 Cut the length of cord slightly shorter than the length of the table, place it on a flat surface, and tie 1 aralia leaf onto the end of the cord with garden string secured in a simple knot.

2 Layer 1 hydrangea leaf stem over the aralia leaf, so its leaves are graduated just below those of the aralia. Wind the string around both stems and cord to make the swag more robust.

Leave the garden string attached to the leaf and cord, as you will be binding all the remaining ingredients onto the rope.

3 Place a group of 3 alchemilla stems on top of the hydrangea and aralia so they form another graduated layer. Pull the string tightly around the first 2 leaf stems before winding more string around all the stems and cord to secure them together.

insider tip

• Mist the flowers and foliage before your guests arrive, so the arrangement looks as fresh as possible.

> Evenly space each layered ingredient, so there are no obvious gaps in between them and none are hidden.

> Continue to layer the ingredients in the same way, so they are evenly distributed and their stems all point in the same direction.

4 Add a pink hydrangea to the garland, placing it just beneath the lime-green alchemilla. Bind it to the secured stems by winding the string 3–4 times around all the stems and the cord, and adjusting the flower head so it is slightly angled to one side of the design.

5 Add another hydrangea leaf stem and a cluster of 3 alchemilla stems to the garland in the same way. Arrange another hydrangea flower at an opposite angle to the first flower.

> Sit the hydrangea head slightly off centre, as it looks more attractive arranged in this way and increases the three-dimensional effect.

6 Add more flowers and foliage until 15cm (6in) of rope remains. Lay the last stems of alchemilla and hydrangea leaf, and, finally, the second aralia leaf, in the opposite direction to the other stems. Pull the string tight and wind it 3–4 times around these last stems and rope. Secure the string firmly in a knot and cut off the ball of string.

Useful Addresses

You should be able to find the flowers used in this book in your local florists or pick them from your garden, but here are some useful addresses – websites, shops, and markets – that we recommend. Also listed here are floristry societies and organizations.

Societies and Organizations

Here is a range of resources that offers information about all plants and flowers, and societies and courses.

British Florist Association, UK
www.britishfloristassociation.org
Floristry trade association with a website directory of florists available in your local area.

Florist & Wholesale Buyer, UK
www.fandwb.com
Trade magazine for the flower industry.

Flowers & Plants Association, UK
www.flowers.org.uk
Information and advice on flowers, plants, seasonal availability, flowers for weddings, and suppliers.

National Association of Flower Arrangement Societies (NAFAS), UK
www.nafas.org.uk
Association that produces a quarterly magazine, has an online shop, and provides contact details for local flower-arranging clubs throughout the UK.

The Royal Horticultural Society, UK
www.rhs.org.uk
For information about all flowers and plants.

Floral Art School of Australia and International Floral Design School, Melbourne, Australia
www.floral-art-school.com.au
For courses, florist's tips, and supplies.

Pearsons School of Floristry Sydney, Australia
www.pearsonsschool.com.au
For a range of courses in floristry.

Flower Markets

Check opening times before you visit flower markets and get there early to beat the rush.

Bernard Street Flower Market, UK
Bernard Street
Southampton SO14 2NS

Columbia Road Flower Market, UK
www.columbiaroad.info/
Columbia Road,
London E2 7QB
Street flower market on Sundays only.

Market Precinct Flower Market, UK
Market Precinct
Pershore Street
Birmingham B5 6UW

New Covent Garden Market, UK
www.newcoventgardenmarket.com
Whoesale market for a wide variety of fresh cut flowers, plants, and sundries.

New Smithfield Market, UK
Whitworth Street East
Oppenshaw
Manchester M11 2WJ

Something Special, UK
www.somethingspecialwholesale.co.uk
Wholesale flower market that also sells sundries.

Queen Victoria Market, Melbourne, Australia
www.qvm.com.au
Open-air market with stalls for cut flowers.

Sydney Flower Market, Australia
www.sydneymarkets.com.au/flower/overview.html
Australia's largest flower market.

Florists and Supplies

Florists often stock a range of supplies as well as fresh flowers. Ask your florist for what you're looking for and they should be able to help.

Bloomsbury Flowers, UK
www.bloomsburyflowers.co.uk
For flowers, floral foam, and wires.

Easy Florists Supplies, UK
www.easyfloristsupplies.co.uk
Online shop for vases, floral foam, ribbon, wire, and other materials.

Floral Essential, UK
www.floralessential.co.uk
For floral foam, containers, tools and equipment, and sundries.

Rainbow Florist Supplies, UK
www.rainbowfloristsupplies.co.uk
Wide variety of all flower arranging sundries.

Fleurus, Queensland, Australia
www.fleurus.com.au
For a range of fresh flowers.

Florists Supplies, Kilburn, Australia
www.floristsuppliers.com.au
For a floral foam, ribbon, and other materials.

Grandiflora, Sydney, Australia
http://grandiflora.net
For a range of fresh flowers.

HE Koch & Co, Melbourne and Sydney, Australia
www.koch.com.au
For floral foam, equipment, and containers.

Flowers Vasette, Melbourne, Australia
www.flowersvasette.com.au
For a range of fresh flowers.

Woodstock Florist Supplies, Australia
www.floristsupplies.com.au
Online supplies for all materials and equipment.

Homeware Shops

Shops you'd usually think of for decorating a home also stock a range of containers and wires that are useful for floristry.

Habitat, UK
www.habitat.co.uk
For vases and other containers.

Heals, UK
www.heals.co.uk
For vases and other containers.

Ikea, UK
www.ikea.com/gb/en
Range of utility glassware and containers.

Ikea, Australia
www.ikea.com/au

LSA, UK
www.lsa-international.com
Large assortment of glassware and ceramics.

Mangan Antiques, UK
www.antiques-trade-warehouse.co.uk
Specialist in Italian, French, and English containers, and decorative items.

Over The Garden Wall, UK
www.otgw.co.uk
Online supplier for old and interesting metal and terracotta containers.

Market Import, Melbourne, Australia
www.marketimport.com
For a range of Mexican glassware and pottery.

Minimax, Melbourne, Australia
www.minimax.com.au
For designer and gift vases.

RG Madden, Melbourne and Sydney, Australia
www.rgmadden.com.au
For designer vases.

Index

Acknowledgments

About the authors

Award-winning florists Mark Welford and Stephen Wicks opened their flower shop, Bloomsbury Flowers, in 1994. Their mission was to make their arrangements as theatrical as possible, but also to keep them simple and classic. Mark and Stephen believe that, even with the most modest bunch of flowers, it's entirely possible to create something gorgeous.

The "Bloomsbury Boys" work with many high-profile clients, including the Royal Opera House, Firmdale Hotels, which have hotels in London and New York, and many venues in and around London.

The authors would like to thank:

The wonderful team at Bloomsbury Flowers for all their help and support, and for keeping the shop running smoothly while we were battling with the blooms on location.

Susannah Steel, for again helping us make sense of everything, and Jessie for her calm support, except when there was a cat about.

Our fantastic photographers, Carolyn Barber and Kate Davis, who were very patient and made our flowers look even more gorgeous.

The team at DK; Peggy Vance, for asking us to work on a second book, Karen Constanti, Dawn Henderson, Christine Keilty, and Peter Luff.

DK would like to thank:

Katie Golsby for proofreading, and Sue Bosanko for the index.

NOTE:
Lily pollen is poisonous to cats and dogs, so if you own one, ensure that you remove all the pollen from the lilies before you arrange them.